MW01118635

FAITH, TRUTH, AND FREEDOM

FAITH, TRUTH, AND FREEDOM

THE EXPULSION OF PROFESSOR GERD LÜDEMANN
FROM THE THEOLOGY FACULTY AT GÖTTINGEN
UNIVERSITY

SYMPOSIUM AND DOCUMENTS

Edited by
JACOB NEUSNER

Academic Studies in Religion and the Social Order
Global Publications, Binghamton University
Binghamton, New York
2002

Cover artwork entitled "Happy Family" by Suzanne R. Neusner.

Library of Congress Cataloging-in-Publication Data:

ISBN   1-58684-218-8 (paperback)
         1-58684-219-6 (hardback)

Published and Distributed by:
Academic Studies in Religion and the Social Order
Global Publications, Binghamton University
State University of New York at Binghamton
LNG 99, Binghamton University
Binghamton, New York, USA 13902-6000
Phone: (607) 777-4495 or 777-6104; Fax: (607) 777-6132
E-mail: pmorewed@binghamton.edu
http://ssips.binghamton.edu

Academic Studies in Religion and the Social Order

Publisher: Global Publications, State University of New York, Binghamton
Address: SSIPS, LNG 99, SUNY Binghamton, New York 13902-6000

TABLE OF CONTENTS

LETTERS ON THE FOREGOING ARTICLE

REPLY TO THE FOREGOING ARTICLE

Preface

This documentary record means to facilitate public debate of a signal, significant event in the academic study of religion in the universities of the West. That event is the expulsion of Professor Gerd Lüdemann from the Theology Faculty at the University of Göttingen by reason of the content of his academic writing and lecturing on the history and theology of earliest Christianity. He was expelled from his post as professor of New Testament and assigned a professorship of the history and literature of Early Christianity thereby losing all his academic rights and being forced into a ghetto existence within the theological faculty. The expulsion of a professor from his academic post because of the public consequence of his scholarship for an academic and also a religious body raises a variety of issues for the academy and for the Church as well as for public policy. What is at issue is the academic study of religion and theology, specifically, the possibility of an authentically academic theological enterprise: can religion be studied by the rules of the academy?

We begin with the parochial and move outward. The particular local issues that concern German university faculties' power to certify, in behalf of Church bodies, the teachers for the study of religion in state schools precipitate the crisis in the life of the German Protestant theological faculties embodied in the Lüdemann case. The institutional arrangements among Church, University, State, and Theological faculty are particular to their setting. In this regard, overseas commentary on a local academic, state, and church culture and arrangement is not invited or even comprehending. American and British faculties afford no warmer a welcome to outside comment and criticism than do German ones. Questions of fact intervene as well, as the account of what was said and done on specific occasions shows. The laws, the contracts, the powers assigned to one body by another — these, however, have no counterpart in the USA, Canada, and Britain. Readers of the symposium and complementary papers will see the diversity of opinion, the different ways altogether in which to begin with observers and participants have framed the question of Professor Lüdemann's fate in particular.

But the event vastly transcends the career of one professor of theology and the institutional arrangements peculiar to his own country and Church therein. Its implications pertain not only to a German university but to the place of the academic study of religion and theology in the Western academy. Issues of law, Church-state relations, academic freedom to study and teach and disseminate the results of both — these intertwine. In theory, most participants in the academic study of religion concur that scholarship on religion and theology under academic auspices adheres to those same rules of reason and criticism that govern all University subjects. And the first of these is, a predetermined conclusion is illegitimate; scholarship of an academic character takes its leave from (mere) erudition when it entertains every possibility and its opposite. Scholarship does its work when, the facts having been accurately portrayed, the labor of analysis and interpretation succeeds the activity of description. Mere repetition of information scarcely initiates the enterprise. The foundations of Western civilization rest on the bed-rock of criticism and analysis, the philosophy embodied in all the pure and applied sciences from the beginnings in Greece to the present. So much for the theory of things.

But in the USA and Britain, as much as in Germany, the unfettered pursuit of critical learning wherever it leads finds itself compromised by the politics of academic fields as much as by the culture and established convictions of those that pursue or sponsor those fields, that enterprise. Everyone understands the conflict of power and preferment that shapes academic careers and the consequent shape of knowledge imparted by those careers. But an academic field shaped by its public responsibility, governed by established convictions not subject to criticism and analysis, produces predetermined conclusions, a program of research meant to validate established attitudes and convictions, not to test possibilities of truth. In that context, the Lüdemann affair contains implications that are scarcely adumbrated by framing the matter juridically and institutionally. At stake for the academic study of religion not only in German but in all Western universities is the intellectual integrity of the subject. That means: are there positions that cannot be entertained, propositions that cannot be open-mindedly investigated, by reason of the protected content and institutionally privileged, standing of said positions and propositions?

I hasten to add, not all participants in the symposium and other documents assembled here define what is at stake in terms of academic freedom to learn and to teach truth whatever the consequences for faith. No party to the discussion claims that the Theology Faculty of Göttingen University acted wantonly, beyond all reason, whether intellectual or institutional. The Church participants in the decision and discussion thereof invoke established, arrangements, legitimate, possibly even in the Protestant Churches and Faculties, and the State of Lower Saxony through its Ministry of Culture has sustained the decision of the President of the University of Göttingen made after consultation with faculty of theology. Nor did the Philosophy Faculty come to Professor Lüdemann's side when that body rejected the proposition of finding a place for him in its program. There are, indeed, many readings of what has happened and its implications for public policy, and there are many parties to the dispute, both within Germany and beyond, and beyond Germany, both in the discipline of the academic study of religion and in the theological disciplines of theological seminaries affiliated with universities and free-standing and church-related.

One fact, and one fact alone, is established in this symposium and accompanying documentary record. The expulsion of Professor Lüdemann by the Theological Faculty at Göttingen University represents an international crisis for the academic study of religion and theology under academic auspices. However matters are resolved, the case transcends the persons involved in it. That is why the participants in this book chose to join in the discussion and debate, and that is why the editor hopes readers will pursue the discussion beyond the pages of this book.

Here, I reproduce and also substantially augment the symposium devoted to Professor Lüdemann's case that was published in the April, 2002, issue of the journal *Religion,* edited by Robert Segal, University of Lancaster.

In organizing the *Religion* symposium and this book as well, I wanted to make provision for a variety of viewpoints and analysis. In preparation, to elicit as wide a range of opinion as I could assemble, I invited the participation of every professor of Theology at the University of Göttingen. Alas, none responded but the dean. I also wrote to the deans of every German university Protestant Theology Faculty, as well as the deans of many other Central European Theology faculties from Scandinavia to Switzerland; every bishop of the Lutheran Church in the State of Lower Saxony, and many important figures in German theological study, as well as public intellectuals in Germany and in the English-speaking world of the academic study of religion under university auspices. The outcome was the same. Most Americans and British whom I invited did reply, and the vast majority participated in the project. Most of the Germans whom I invited did not bother to reply at all, not the bishops, not the professors, not the deans, except those who participate.

That fact makes me wonder whether the German theological faculties grasp the importance and complexity of the issues inherent in the disposition of Professor Lüdemann's career by his colleagues in Göttingen. The publication of the symposium in *Religion* and this book make it impossible to continue to pretend that in Göttingen in the recent past has happened nothing of consequence for the academic study of religion and theology — nothing that those responsible feel an obligation to explain and justify. In this regard I was glad to include Dean Kratz's response, together with Professor Lüdemann's reply to him.

Newspaper coverage, by contrast, has recognized the matter as consequential. I reproduce only a bit of the more important newspaper comment mainly from Germany but also from the USA, where Lüdemann has taught at Vanderbilt University, as well as other writings devoted to the event.

I owe the title of this book to Professor William Scott Green, University of Rochester.

I thank cordially Academic Press, London, for permission to reprint the symposium originally published by *Religion.* My thanks go also to the colleagues who permitted me to reproduce their writings, as well as to the German periodicals that did the same. The original sources are indicated where they are reproduced, and all are reprinted with permission of the copyright holder and author. All parties to the debate have cooperated to secure this public hearing for the several positions and readings of what is at stake. That is a credit to everyone represented in these pages.

In addition to this symposium and documentary record, I have arranged for the Global Press publication in English of Professor Lüdemann's systematic statement of the matter and the issues that in here as he sees them. This is *Im Würgegriff der Kirche. Für die Freiheit der theologischen Wissenschaft.* Lüneburg 1998: zu Klampen-Verlag.

In bringing into print the Religion Symposium and the two Global Publications volumes I hope to underscore the importance of what has happened as well as to facilitate debate on issues of public policy that are intertwined in the response of the Göttingen Theology Faculty to the issues raised by Professor Lüdemann's scholarly writings about earliest Christianity and its history other fundamental issues of culture, religion, and theology. These concern the academic study of religion and theology, the relationship of Church and University, and religious faith and academic freedom: Lehrfreiheit and Lernfreiheit, the foundations of intellectual integrity in the academy.

Jacob Neusner

Research Professor of Religion and Theology
Bard College
Annandale-on-Hudson NY 12572
neusner@webjogger.net

Contributors

Prof. Dr. Dr. Gerhard Besier graduated in theology and history, and specialised in modern church history. His latest published work is *Die Kirchen und das Dritte Reich. Vol.3: Spaltungen und Abwehrkämpfe 1934–1937*, Berlin-Munich: Ullstein-Propyläen 2001 (1262 pp.).

Bruce Chilton is Bernard Iddings Bell Professor of Religion at Bard College and Rector of the Church of St John the Evangelist.

Robert W. Funk is Founder of the Jesus Seminar and Director of Westar Institute.

Douglas A. Knight is Professor of Hebrew Bible and Chair of the Graduate Department of Religion of Vanderbilt University, Nashville, Tennessee. He received his Dr. theol. from Georg-August-Universität in Göttingen, in 1973.

Reinhard G. Kratz is Dean of the Theological Faculty of Georg- August-Universität in Göttingen and Professor of Old Testament. His latest published work is *Die Komposition der erzählenden Bücher des Alten Testaments*, Göttingen: Vandenhoeck & Ruprecht 2000 (336 pp.).

Bernhard Lang teaches Old Testament and religious studies at the University of Paderborn, Germany, and at the University of St. Andrews, Scotland. Religious affiliation: Roman Catholic. Recent publications: *Sacred Games* (1997), *Heaven: A History* (with Colleen McDannell, 2d ed. 2001), *The Hebrew God* (2002), all with Yale University Press.

Amy-Jill Levine is E. Rhodes and Leona B. Carpenter Professor of New Testament Studies at Vanderbilt University Divinity School and Graduate Department of Religion, Nashville, Tennessee.

Gerd Lüdemann is Professor of the History and Literature of Early Christianity at the University of Göttingen. His latest published work is *Paulus, der Gründer des Christentums*, Lüneburg: zu Klampen 2001 (270 pp.) /*Paul – The Founder of Christianity*, Amherst: Prometheus Books 2002.

Jacob Neusner is Research Professor of Religion and Theology at Bard College, Annandale-on-Hudson, New York.

Stephen B. Presser is the Raoul Berger Professor of Legal History at Northwestern University School of Law, a Professor of Business Law at Northwestern University's Kellogg School of Management, an Associate Research Fellow at the Institute of United States Studies of the University of London, and the Legal Affairs Editor for Chronicles: A Magazine of American Culture. Professor Presser is the author of *Recapturing the Constitution: Race Religion and Abortion Reconsidered* (Washington, D.C., Regnery Publishing, 1994), the senior co-author of *Law and Jurisprudence in American History* (St. Paul, West Group, 4th ed. 2000), and the co-author, with Douglas W. Kmiec, of *The American Constitutional Order: History Cases and Philosophy* (Cincinnati, Anderson Publishing, 1998).

Robert Price is Professor of Biblical Criticism, Center for Inquiry Institute, Amherst, NY and Editor, *Journal of Higher Criticism*.

Professor of American Christianity in Saint Louis since 1991, William Shea also taught at the Catholic University of America and The University of South Florida. His books include *The Naturalists and the Supernatural* (1984), *The Struggle over the Past: Fundamentalism in the Modern World* (1993), *Knowledge and Belief in America* (with Peter Huff 1995), and *Trying Times: Catholic Universities in the Twentieth Century* (1999). He has published many essays on theology in the university. He is currently working on a study of American Evangelicals and Roman Catholics.

Daniel Wiebe is Professor of Divinity (Philosophy of Religion) at Trinity College, University of Toronto. His most recent monograph is *The Politics of Religious Studies. The Continuing Conflict with Theology in the Academy.* New York: St. Martin's Press, 1999.

1

The Decline of Academic Theology at Göttingen[1]

Gerd Lüdemann

Abstract: Until recently, the transfer of an academic theologian to another faculty as a result of objections by ecclesiastical officials was limited to Catholic professors. Now for the first time in the annals of the German university, a Protestant professor faces such an action by a church body. Professor Gerd Lüdemann, who since 1983 has taught New Testament Studies in the University of Göttingen, has become the target of criticism by Confederation of Lutheran Churches in Lower Saxony. As a result of a preliminary decision by the president of his University, theology students can no longer receive credit for attending his courses, nor can he serve as director or advisor of graduate studies. Professor Lüdemann tells the story of his censure and describes the present situation which is now before a court of law.

> The natural relationship of theology to religion is not one of friendship, but of hostility. Theology can be called the satan of religion. Theology cannot create a religion but at best supports and strengthens a religion which one has from elsewhere. For that reason it can also contaminate religion. (Overbeck 1995: 580)

After periods of teaching and research at McMaster University (1977-1979) and Vanderbilt University (1979-1982), I have since 1983 held a chair in New Testament Studies in the theological faculty of the University of Göttingen.

---

[1] This article, a thoroughly revised and updated version of the preface to the U.S. edition of my book *The Great Deception* (Lüdemann 1999: IX-XXII), summarizes the events that led to my ongoing dispute with the Confederation of Protestant Churches in Lower Saxony, the Minister of Science and Culture of Lower Saxony and the University of Göttingen. I thank

Since its foundation in 1737, the University of Göttingen has been famous for its interest in history, and that is particularly true of the theology that has originated here. Many of the Göttingen theologians, such as Julius Wellhausen (1844-1918), were pioneers of historical criticism and remain of international importance today: Emil Schürer (1844-1910), Walter Bauer (1877-1960), Joachim Jeremias (1900-1979), Ernst Käsemann (1908-1998), and Hans Conzelmann (1915-1989), to name only a few, also occupied chairs in New Testament Studies in the theological faculty. Then, about a century ago, Göttingen was the source of the so-called History of Religions School, which is again enjoying increased international popularity. Some of the works from this school have only recently been translated into English. Here I would mention only Hermann Gunkel, *The Influence of the Holy Spirit: The Popular View of the Apostolic Age and the Teaching of the Apostle Paul: A Biblical-theological Study* (Gunkel 1888); Johannes Weiss, *Jesus' Proclamation of the Kingdom of God* (Weiss 1892), and William Wrede, *The Messianic Secret in the Gospels* (Wrede 1901).

The History of Religions School[2] is a designation used to denote a group of German Protestant theologians active in the late 19th and early 20th centuries, most of whom were New Testament scholars. Their main conviction was that religion is not something fixed, but an evolving phenomenon subject to human history. The History of Religions School was not a theological school in the sense that it stemmed from an individual whose ideas were taken up and developed. Rather, in a lengthy process of development lasting around fifteen years, it emerged from the shared life and work of young theologians who, beginning in 1886 gained their Habilitations (a second doctorate that a candidate in the German university system must normally complete) primarily in Göttingen. This group centered around Albert Eichhorn (1856-1926) and William Wrede (1859-1906), and included the students Hermann Gunkel (1862-1932), Heinrich Hackmann (1864-1935), Alfred Rahlfs (1865-1935), and Johannes Weiss (1863-1914). They were soon joined by Wilhelm Bousset (1865-1920), Ernst Troeltsch (1865-1923), and Wilhelm Heitmüller (1869-1926). Their uncompromising dedication to the study of early Christian texts from a strictly historical perspective, subject to no dogmatic compulsions, soon led to charges that they were radicals. The effect that their "radicalism" had on students is evident in the following letter by an eyewitness:

> Hardly had I become active when Wilhelm (i.e. Lueken[3]) took
> me for a walk to Rohn's (in Göttingen). On the way he told me that

---

my friend Dr. John Bowden for the original translation and my friend Tom Hall for helping me in matters of updating and revisions.

[2] Cf. Gerd Lüdemann and Alf Özen. "Religionsgeschichtliche Schule", TRE 28 (1997): 618-624.

[3] Wilhelm Lueken (1875-1961) was a pupil and friend of Wilhelm Bousset.

Strauss's *Leben Jesu* [4] was very tame; now people were going much further. I was dumbfounded. The people around Bousset seemed to me to be a horde of iconoclasts who wanted to smash everything to pieces ... Certainly, the elite stuck to Bousset. Just as one misses the creator in Darwin's creation, so I missed the Holy Spirit in Bousset's Bible. It was all human work, and moreover it stank of forgeries. I became very disturbed that the first letter of Peter was said not to have been written by the apostle.[5]

I see myself as being in the tradition of this school and practice a strictly historical exegesis of the New Testament in the framework of the religions of the Hellenistic period. This is evident from monographs on Simon Magus (Lüdemann 1975), the chronology of Paul (Lüdemann 1984), anti-Paulinism in early Christianity (Lüdemann 1989), and a commentary on the historical value of the Acts of the Apostles (Lüdemann 1989) which have brought me international recognition. But in the course of my investigation of the resurrection of Jesus (Lüdemann 1994), of the heretics in early Christianity (Lüdemann 1996), of the unholy in Holy Scripture (Lüdemann 1997), of the virgin birth (Lüdemann 1998) and finally, in *Jesus after 2000 Years* (Lüdemann 2001), of the many words and actions of Jesus which have been put into his mouth or attributed to him only at a later stage, I have come to the following conclusion: My previous faith, derived as it was from the biblical message, has become impossible. This is so not only because its points of reference, above all the resurrection of Jesus, have proved invalid, but also because the person of Jesus himself becomes insufficient as a foundation of faith once most of the New Testament statements about him have proved to be later interpretations by the community. Jesus deceived himself in expecting the kingdom of God. Instead the church arrived; and it not only recklessly changed the message of Jesus, but also in numerous cases turned that distorted doctrine against the very Judaism from which it sprang.

When I made public the consequences of my historical insights and said goodbye to Christianity with a "Letter to Jesus" (Lüdemann 1999: 1-9), the Confederation of Protestant Churches in Lower Saxony applied to my superior, the Minister of Science and Culture of Lower Saxony, and called for my discharge from my professorship, an action which would have taken away my livelihood. After that request had failed, the same body of church officials called for my

---

[4]David Friedrich Strauss's (1808-1874) work *Das Leben Jesu* (2 vols, 1835-1836; second edition 1838-1839), famously translated by George Eliot, reissued as The Life of Jesus critically Examined, ed. Peter C. Hodgson (Minneapolis: Fortress Press, 1972, and London: SCM Press, 1973), was basic reading for the history-of-religions school. Rudolf Bultmann still planned to dedicate the first edition of his book *Die Geschichte der synoptischen Tradition* (*The History of the Synoptic Tradition*, 1921) to the memory of D. F. Strauss, but refrained from doing so for tactical reasons.

[5]Letter from Karl Woebcken to Emil Lueken, 25 May 1956 (Lüdemann Archive).

immediate dismissal from the theological faculty.[6] Under pressure from the church, my own colleagues, the members of the Göttingen Theological Faculty, endorsed this request in two statements. The first, published on 27 April 1998, reads as follows:

> At the invitation of the Dean, on 22 April 1998 an extraordinary session of the Collegium of Professors of the Theological Faculty of Göttingen was held at which Professor Lüdemann explained his public statements about his "renunciation" of Christianity. Subsequently the members of the Collegium present unanimously passed the following resolution:
>
> We respect the personal decisions which stand behind Professor Lüdemann's statements. However, we dispute that these statements are the necessary conclusions to be drawn from scientific insights. Although our teaching and research as professors of the theological faculty differs widely, we hold Christian faith and science to be essentially compatible. It is also one of the tasks of the theological faculty to train future pastors and teachers of religion with scholarly responsibility in accordance with the principles of the Protestant churches. Therefore, we call upon Professor Lüdemann to reflect upon his membership in the theological faculty, going beyond considerations of personal expediency and practicing the truthfulness that he always calls for. In our view, in making statements of his kind, Professor Lüdemann is in flagrant conflict with the character and tasks of a theological faculty.

The second resolution, addressed to the President of the university, was composed on 19 November 1998 and reads thus:

> At the session of the professors of the theological faculty of Göttingen on 18 November 1998 it was resolved:
>
> 1. In that Professor Dr. G. Lüdemann has fundamentally put in question the intrinsic soundness of Protestant theology at the university, he has terminated his membership in the faculty of Protestant theology ...
>
> Consequently, the professors have passed the following resolution:
>
> Point 1 gives rise to serious objections to Professor Lüdemann's continuing membership in the theological faculty. The teachers therefore recommend that the President work toward the

---

[6] I deal with this conflict separately in my book *Im Würgegriff der Kirche. Für die Freiheit der theologischen Wissenschaft* (In the Stranglehold of the Church. Toward the Freedom of Theological Science) (Lüneburg: zu Klampen Verlag, 1998). Since the publication of that book I have had the opportunity to read my personal files and the correspondence between my attorney and the University of Göttingen, in which I found a reference to the initial attempt of the church to have me fired.

incorporation of his chair into another faculty. The professors are concerned to arrive at a solution which makes it possible for Professor Lüdemann to continue his scholarly work.

This resolution was passed with fifteen votes in favor and one abstention.

The dispute has been placed in abeyance until the present by a letter from the President of the University of Göttingen dated 17 December 1998. After the philosophy faculty had declined to incorporate my chair into its faculty, the President's letter provisionally confirmed my membership in the theology faculty – a step the Ministry of Science and Culture on February 4, 1999 provisionally endorsed. The provisional character has to be noted, for it was put in there to give the Confederation of Churches in Lower Saxony time to examine issues of law.[7]

At the same time my previous chair in New Testament was renamed and is now a chair in the "History and Literature of Early Christianity." The aim of this renaming is, on the one hand, to remove me from the training of pastors and teachers of protestant religion in the theological faculties, and on the other, to continue to guarantee the freedom of research to which I have a right, protected by law, as a professor of theology appointed by the state.

As a further step in the realignment of chairs and duties, the Ministry of Science and Culture in Lower Saxony has established a new chair for New Testament in the theological faculty in Göttingen in order to meet the conditions of the treaty between the churches of the Confederation of Protestant Churches in Lower Saxony and the state. Whether the Confederation (which after failing to make the University fire me on disciplinary grounds had called for my immediate withdrawal from the theological faculty) is in agreement with this solution remains to be seen.

My own faculty regards this solution as a make-shift solution ("Notlösung") (Busch 1999) which was necessary because I did not leave the faculty voluntarily. I for my part have taken the matter to court; for the action of the President as promising as it looks on the surface, has actually deprived me of my academic rights. (Let me hasten to add that I failed twice in my attempt to get injunctions against the decision of the University of Göttingen.) The new area that I teach is part of no curriculum and consequently offers no degrees whatsoever. I was invited to develop a curriculum, but I am less than enthusiastic about doing so under the shadow of that double proviso, the more so, since the decision has already been made not to replace me after my regular retirement in 2011. In addition, the church would have the right to lodge an objection to such a curriculum within the theological faculty. Further, I am explicitly denied academic rights in my previous

---

[7]In the meantime, the expert opinion which the Confederation of Churches had ordered has now been published in a German periodical of Law. It is Rainer Mainusch. 'Lehrmäßige Beanstandung eines evangelischen Theologieprofessors', Die Öffentliche Verwaltung, August 1999, Heft 16, 677-685. The author argues that the University *must* transfer me to another faculty.

discipline, "New Testament", for New Testament is, I am told, a theological discipline whereas my new area "History and Literature of Early Christianity," is not. Finally, the written contract that I have with the University of Göttingen has been made void by the renaming of my chair in New Testament. As a consequence my research money has been cut in half and the position of an assistant which corresponds to an Assistant professor in the English speaking world has been taken away from me. The result of these actions is that no students attend my classes, the academic theological guild in Germany avoids me, and my doctoral students will have a hard time finding other supervisors. No doubt because of the near-absurdity of the situation, a previous dean of my faculty has publicly defended the myth that neither the church nor the University nor my faculty started the whole process that led to the actions against me; rather it was the Ministry of Science and Culture that, after reading my statements, came to the conclusion that I could no longer teach New Testament studies in a theological faculty (Busch 1999; Mühlenberg 2000). The same story was included by the dean and his successor in their response (Funk 2000b; Besier 2000) to a public letter by the Jesus Seminar in my support. (Funk 2000a). Let me plainly state that their assertion is untrue. The action was started by the Confederation of Lutheran Churches in Lower Saxony by a letter of April 17, 1998 to the Ministry of Science and Culture. The deans of my faculty must have known this. Why are they not telling the truth? Furthermore, two pieces of information are important to understand the whole process. First, in the aforementioned letter of April 17 the church officials deem it necessary for the faculty of theology to address my case. That was done on the meeting of April 22 (see above). Second, the official objection to my continued service as a professor at the theological faculty was sent to the Ministry of Science and Culture November 2, 1998.

At this point some information must be given about the nature of the complex legal status of theological faculties in Germany.

Treaties between the state and the Christian churches guarantee the existence of these theological faculties in Germany. The theological faculties are responsible for the training not only of future pastors, but also of teachers of religion, since in German schools the Protestant and Catholic religions are regular subjects of study. Anyone who wants to pass a theological examination must be a baptized member of one of the major Christian denominations. The same is also true for future professors. Whereas in the Catholic sphere a call to a professorship is possible only if the church gives its assent, the treaties between the Protestant churches and the state recognize no veto corresponding to the Catholic right. The treaties between the Protestant churches and the state differ from the corresponding agreements on the Catholic side in the further detail that it is no longer possible to object to a professor after his appointment. So in the Catholic sphere there have been, and are, quite a number of subsequent objections to professors (the best-known case is that of Hans Küng), which result in a transfer of the professor concerned to another faculty and a new appointment to the chair of a professor more acceptable to the church. All that was previously unknown in the Protestant sphere; my case is the first of its kind in the history of the Protestant theological faculties in Germany.

I regard as artificial the strict denominational division within academic theology, and also the close connection between theology and the church, which goes with it. In my view it is an intrinsic contradiction for academic theology on the one hand to claim for itself the epithet "scientific" and on the other hand to subserve the goals and principles of the church. Of course, the amalgamation of the church and academic theology in the Protestant sphere has been a long time in the making. Only recently (1995), an oath dating from the year 1848 was reintroduced into my faculty after a lapse of some thirty years. Since then any newly appointed professor and any new lecturer must take the following oath: "I commit myself to presenting the theological disciplines honestly, clearly and thoroughly in agreement with the principles of the Evangelical Lutheran church." In my view, to tie theology to the church in this way goes against its claim to be a scientific, or even a truly academic discipline.

This bond with the church is also abundantly clear in the statement by my colleagues quoted above. Note what they say of my "renunciation" of Christianity:

> We dispute that these statements are the necessary conclusions
> to be drawn from scientific insights. Although our teaching and research
> as professors of the theological faculty differ widely, we hold Christian
> faith and science to be essentially compatible.

From a purely scholarly perspective, the following serious objections to this statement arise:

First, the contents of the scientific insights that have led me to "renounce" Christianity have been neither discussed nor even adduced.

Second, the statement that faith and science are essentially compatible needs to be complemented by a statement about the result of my scientific investigation of Christianity, which is the issue here. Instead of this, my colleagues claim in advance something that needs to be proved. This fatal error recalls a sentence from the Catholic Anti-Modernist Oath of 1910:

> At the same time I reject the error of those who claim that the
> faith presented by the church could conflict with history and that the
> Catholic dogmas ... cannot be made to accord with the real origin of the
> Christian religion (Mulert 1911: 43).[8]

---

[8]The Latin text reads thus: *Idem reprobo errorem affirmantium, propositam ab Ecclesia fidem posse historiae repugnare, et catholica dogmata, quo sensu nunc intelliguntur cum verioribus christianae religionis originibus componi non posse.*

Thus the key issue is not the general one of whether Christian faith and scholarship are essentially compatible, but the concrete one of whether belief in the resurrection of Jesus is today compatible with the fact that Jesus' body was not raised, but underwent natural decay.

In this connection it would be useful to recall Max Weber's classic article "On the Inner Call to Scholarship" (Weber 1968: 311-339). This rightly states, "Any theology requires some specific assumptions which justify its conclusions " (Weber 1968: 336). A little later Weber aptly remarks that any theology which wants to remain true to itself calls for the sacrifice of the intellect, simply because it must presuppose "revelation." For the great sociologist, "such a sacrifice of the intellect in favor of an unconditional religious surrender ... is morally something quite different from that avoidance of the simple intellectual obligation to honesty which arises when one does not have the courage to become clear about one's own ultimate position, but makes this obligation easier by weak relativization" (Weber 1968: 338f.).

Unless I have mistaken them completely, the statement made by my colleagues is guilty of the last charge, or comes suspiciously close to it. Is not the bland affirmation that Christian faith and science are essentially compatible an avoidance of the obligation to be honest? As is the case with Max Weber, most scholars regard it impossible for traditional Christian faith and science to be reconciled without a sacrifice of the intellect.

To be sure, my colleagues avowed respect for my decisions, but at the same time called on me to go beyond personal expediency and to reflect on my own membership in the theological faculty, practicing the truthfulness that I call for. To be specific, they wanted me to leave the faculty voluntarily. As I did not do this, six months later, under increased pressure from the church, they sent a recommendation to the President of the university to remove my chair from the theological faculty.

Their charge that I had employed a tactical maneuver relates to my statement that I wanted to continue to remain in the theological faculty but no longer as a Christian professor. This decision is based on my firm intention to bring to bear the best traditions of free Protestant theology and to reestablish the critical principle within the confessional theological faculties, which have become so compliant as to be anemic. My colleagues evidently do not recognize the possible tension, not to say the possible contradiction, between scientific judgments and judgments of faith. For in their view only those may belong to the faculty who can accept the basic doctrines of the Christian tradition.

I regard this as a preliminary decision which it is improper for a scholar to make, and which in the last resort derives from Roman Catholic thinking (see the above text on the Anti-Modernist Oath).

At the same time it should be remarked that in their research and teaching, most of my colleagues have long since left the principles of the church behind them but (seek to) attach themselves to this tradition by symbolic interpretation and other interpretative skills. Hardly one of them shares the eschatological presuppositions of the church's tradition, and very few expect, for example, the return of Christ in judgment. To keep quiet about this could similarly be described as personal expediency.

So it is high time to talk about theology and its content, and that requires a discussion about the historical foundations of Christian faith – without any tactics, posturings, or evasions – even at the risk of having openly to repudiate the principles of the Evangelical Church or other confessional writings. Unless the confessional beliefs of the churches can be objectively examined, theology cannot claim to possess the intellectual integrity of an academic discipline. The corollary question poses itself: Does theology which is in the service of the church/synagogue/mosque belong in the universities at all? Can the results of scholarship be trusted when there are preconditions to the conclusions you can reach and publicize?

For now, the academic study of religion in German universities is almost entirely in the hands of social science or philology. The academic study of religion one finds in the English speaking world and in other parts of Europe – not philology or philosophy, but honest and unblinking examination of religion – hardly exists in German universities. Furthermore what theology many of them do offer has an exclusively Christian orientation, either Protestant or Catholic. This is not surprising because the chairs that are located in theological faculties need the assent of the church officials. Despite the pretenses of the confessional theologians, a religious studies program offering genuine breadth of scope, solid scholarly foundations, and true academic freedom is to all intents and purposes practically non-existent in German Universities.

As long as theology remains in the university, it has to research and inform, not reveal and preach; to bring people to maturity in matters of religion, not lead them astray into servitude to an old superstition, no matter how modern it may claim to be. To paraphrase Theodor Mommsen (1817-1903), theology must remain a relentlessly honest investigation of the truth, evading no doubts, and papering over no gaps in the tradition. A remark by Bertrand Russell still applies without qualification to its maturing and ongoing development:

> Even if the open windows of science at first make us shiver
> with cold after the cosy indoor warmth of traditional humanizing myths,
> in the end the fresh air brings vigour, and the great spaces have a
> splendour of their own (Russell 1957: 43).

BIBLIOGRAPHY

Preliminary note: The articles by Besier 2000, Busch 1999, Funk 2000a and 2000b, and Mühlenberg 2000 along with other documents related to my case can be read at my website: www.gerdluedemann.de in the section *Aktuelles*.

Besier, Gerhard. 'Wie zivilisierte Menschen üblicherweise verkehren:Welche Öffentlichkeit? Die Göttinger Theologen verbitten sich im Fall Lüdemann amerikanische Kollegenkritik'. In: *Die Welt*, June 7, *2000*.

Busch, Eberhard. 'Erklärung des Dekans zur Entscheidung hinsichtlich der künftigen akademischen Stellung von Prof. Dr. Gerd Lüdemann'. February 10, *1999*.

Funk, Robert W. *Letter of Concern for Prof. Dr. Gerd Luedemann*, March 21, *2000a*.

Funk, Robert W. *Second Letter on Behalf of Prof. Dr. Gerd Luedemann*, June 30, *2000b*.

Gunkel, Hermann. *Die Wirkungen des heiligen Geistes*. Göttingen: Vandenhoeck & Ruprecht, *1888* (E.T.: *The Influence of the Holy Spirit: The Popular View of the Apostolic Age and the Teaching of the Apostle Paul: A Biblical.Theological Study*; translated by Roy A. Harrisville and Philip A. Quanbeck II. Philadelphia: Fortress Press, 1979).

Lüdemann, Gerd. *Untersuchungen zur simonianischen Gnosis*. Göttingen: Vandenhoeck & Ruprecht, *1975*.

Lüdemann, Gerd. *Paul, Apostle to the Gentiles, Studies in Chronology*. Minneapolis: Fortress Press, and London: SCM Press, *1984*.

Lüdemann, Gerd. *Opposition to Paul in Jewish Christianity*. Minneapolis: Fortress Press, *1989*

Lüdemann, Gerd. *Early Christianity According to the Traditions in Acts: A Commentary*, London: SCM Press, and Minneapolis: Fortress Press, *1989*.

Lüdemann, Gerd. *The Resurrection of Jesus: History, Experience, Theology*, London: SCM Press, and Minneapolis: Fortress Press, *1994*.

Lüdemann, Gerd. Heretics: *The Other Side of Early Christianity*, London: SCM Press, and Louisville: Westminster John Knox Press, *1996*.

Lüdemann, Gerd. *The Unholy in Holy Scripture: The Dark Side of the Bible*, London: SCM Press, and Louisville: Westminster John Knox Press, *1997*.

Lüdemann, Gerd. *Virgin Birth? The Real Story of Mary and Her Son Jesus.* London: SCM Press, and Harrisburg, Pa.: Trinity Press International, *1998*.

Lüdemann, Gerd. *The Great Deception: And what Jesus really said and did.* London: SCM Press, 1998, and Amherst, N.Y.: Prometheus Books, *1999*.

Lüdemann, Gerd. *Jesus after Two Thousand Years: What he really said and did*, London: SCM Press, 2000, and Amherst, N.Y.: Prometheus Books, *2001*.

Mulert, Hermann. *Anti-Modernisten-Eid, freie Forschung und theologische Fakultäten. Mit Anhang: Der Anti-Modernisteneid, lateinisch und deutsch nebst Aktenstücken.* Halle: Verlag des Evangelischen Bundes, *1911*.

Overbeck, Franz. *Werke und Nachlass. Vol. 5 of Kirchenlexicon. Texte. Ausgewählte Artikel J-Z*, Stuttgart/Weimar: Verlag J. B. Metzler, *1995*.

Russell, Bertrand. 'What I believe', in: *Why I am not a Christian and other Essays Essays on Religion and Other Related Subjects*, edited by Paul Edwards, New York: Simon and Schuster, *1957*.

Weber, Max. *Soziologie. Wissenschaftliche Analysen. Politik,* 4. Auflage, Stuttgart: Alfred Kröner Verlag, *1968,* 311-339.

Weiss, Johannes. *Die Predigt Jesu vom Reiche Gottes,* Göttingen: Vandenhoeck & Ruprecht, *1892* (E.T. *Jesus' Proclamation of the Kingdom of God*, edited by Richard Hyde Hiers and David Larrimore Holland, Philadelphia: Fortress Press, and London: SCM Press, 1971).

Wrede, William. *Das Messiasgeheimnis in den Evangelien.* Göttingen: Vandenhoeck & Ruprecht, *1901* (E.T. *The Messianic Secret in the Gospels.* Cambridge: James Clarke 1971.)

2

A Professor of Theology
Is No "Normal' University Teacher:"
On a Changed "Basis of Relations"

Gerhard Besier
University of Heidelberg

Since the Göttingen professor of New Testament Gerd Lüdemann had dissociated himself from the Christian belief, the German courts he appealed to decided that the 'basis of relations' valid when he signed his contract with the University, was changed by Lüdemann himself. The courts also stated that he should have expected the consequences which followed. Lüdemann has held a special status at the school of theology until the present day, and the change of name of his Chair to "History and literature of early Christianity", according to German judges, is as right as the cuts regarding finances and personnel. Furthermore, he must accept the fact that he is no longer allowed to examine students or take part in projects regarding doctoral dissertations or *Habilitationen* (postdoctoral lecturing qualifications).

In 1999, the administrative court of Göttingen stated in its opinion that a professor of theology is a civil servant, but in contrast to a "'normal' University professor," his appointment 'depends on the further ecclesiastical condition that he belong to the denomination in question and be accepted by the church in question. Thus his office is a so-called denomination-bound state office.' In this context, it was 'only a job of the [...] church, not of the religiously and ideologically neutral *Land* Niedersachsen, to decide' whether the person in question 'is authorised to represent the theology of this confession'. Not only at the point of time of the appointment, but also anytime later might a church, due to its right of self-determination, complain about the research and teachings of a professor. In such a case, the state, 'due to the integrity of an ecclesiastical confession protected by the

Constitution, [is] *obliged* to attend to' the fact that a no longer authorised teacher, researcher and examinator will no longer act as such.

It was clear to the court that the church did not want to accept a teacher who 'in core points supports a theory causing its audience – insofar as they will be pastors of the confederate Protestant Church – to receive an official flogging, should they follow their teacher.'

This way of arguing, though, leaves no doubt that the court has hardly an idea of the real situation in Protestant theological schools. Especially in the historical area, chair holders often work purely with methods of religious science or religious sociology. Personal beliefs of the teachers hardly play any role at all. One may regret or welcome this, according to one's personal opinion, but in any case, these are the facts. Neither must anyone commit themselves to the Bible or to a confession when they are appointed. A future teacher of theology needs not even have passed the second Church exam. Thus, he (or rarely, she) may educate prospective pastors without ever having worked in this field himself. The only condition for an appointment is being a formal member of one of the Protestant churches which developed from the former state churches. Only exceptionally may members of a Free Church be appointed.

While in Scandinavian countries and in Great Britain confessionally bound theological schools are constantly giving way to multi-confessional places of education carrying the additional remark 'and religious studies', both German mainstream churches insist on the currently valid state-church legislation. But here too, during the past eighty years the 'basis of relations' has changed. A good third of the Federal German population does not belong to either folk church, but must finance the education of confessionally bound pastors and religious education teachers with their taxes. The number of students of theology has diminished by half during the past ten years. Although there has been this dramatic decrease, a financially drained state must go on supporting all schools of theology – even in double number in some places, although the historical subjects in the courses of studies of Protestant or Catholic theology hardly differ at all nowadays. Contemporarily, the number of students in German Universities continues growing, and some 'crowd courses' would seriously need more teachers. But a transfer of a number of chairs from theology to those courses is not being done: there are guarantees for those chairs. Instead of cutting down the number of professoral chairs of theology, the *Land* Niedersachsen appointed a further professor for the school of theology of the University of Göttingen – as a compensation for Lüdemann, who was no longer accepted by his church. The 'case' Lüdemann might become a 'case of schools of theology'. If the general public should become interested in this problem, the business partners state and church might have to consider a re-evaluation of the regarding state-church arrangements.

3

Bruce D. Chilton

Bard College

Professor Lüdemann's account of his contentious reassignment at the University of Göttingen makes me feel sympathy for him, but his own position also surprises me. Basically, I am surprised that he was surprised by what happened. His description has it that he decided to say "goodbye" to Christianity:

> When I made public the consequences of my historical insights and said goodbye to Christianity with a "Letter to Jesus" (Lüdemann 1999: 1-9), the Confederation of Protestant Churches in Lower Saxony applied to my superior, the Minister of Science and Culture of Lower Saxony, and called for my discharge from my professorship...

Aufwiedersehen need not imply a definitive departure. Although it seems to do so here, one might depart from "Christianity," a term which derives from the reference of outsiders (so Acts 11:26) to Jesus' followers as "groupies for Christ," in the hope of return to the faith Jesus promoted within his own terms of reference. That, indeed, is a characteristically Protestant move, implicit in the work, say, of Adolf von Harnack, Albert Schweitzer, Rudolf Bultmann, and Willi Marxsen.

Luther's embrace of St Paul's justification *sola gratia* characterizes Protestantism to this day, but since the eighteenth century Protestant intellectuals have been engaged in an additional project. They have investigated Jesus in order to reform Christianity, and the work of the scholars just named makes that explicit. Their influence has resulted in re-evaluations of Christology, which may seem, whether for believing or non-believing observers, to be needless exercises in academic radicalism. But the logic of the movement is plain: "the historical Jesus" has never been merely historical, which is why the topic enjoys asymmetrical attention from the point of view of the understanding of the New Testament. Even (perhaps especially) when no theological motivation for the study of Jesus is claimed, all of the findings of any quest to date inextricably involve theological considerations and theological conclusions.

Saying that is not to fault any such work; the point — a commonplace in the study of the new Testament — is that the Gospels were produced for faith and within faith, and are not historical, at least not as "history" is commonly understood. A scholar might infer from their testimony what Jesus did and said to produce the faith him which the texts attest, but that process of literary inference will have to include an assessment of the theologies embedded within the texts, within any sources postulated, and among Jesus' followers, as well as those attributable to Jesus himself. True, some interpreters wish to revert to what I call the Sgt. Joe Friday approach to the Bible: "Nothing but the facts, ma'am." Fortunately, our textual witnesses do not have to follow the script of "Dragnet." The Gospels do not sob, look up, and change their tune to suit our desire for literal history.

Professor Lüdemann's name could easily be added after Willi Marxsen's, both in his detailed contributions and in his sensitivity to the theological dimension of his scholarly work. Marxsen's famously controversial resumé of the significance of the resurrection, *Die Sache Jesu geht weiter* (translatable — however imperfectly — as "Jesus' cause goes on") receives an elegant explication with new twists and textures in Lüdemann's more detailed study.

When you take a position such as this, people who react on the basis of received Christianity often complain that the very substance of their faith is challenged. Marxsen and Lüdemann have been accused of reductionism, and such criticism has sometimes been intemperate and ill considered. The present writer has been accused of blasphemy for arguing that the resurrection is best understood within the context of the visionary, meditative discipline of Jesus and his disciples. No one can enjoy vilification of that kind, especially when it comes from putative scholars saying they are guided by their adherence to the teachings of Jesus.

But this underlying dynamic, however unpleasant to those who explore original ideas within the context of contemporary Christianity, is by now routine. The intensity of reaction is often magnified by the crudity of the rhetoric involved, and the bureaucratic language deployed by the theological faculty at Göttingen to address the issue of Prof. Lüdemann's leave-taking of Christianity is a case in point:

> In that Professor Dr. G. Lüdemann has fundamentally put in
> question the intrinsic soundness of Protestant theology at the university,
> he has terminated his membership in the faculty of Protestant theology...

This is an odd way to say you are removing someone from your group; the apparent aim is to accept as little responsibility as possible. Passive-aggressive gambits such as these help to flag the unreflective roots of these reactions. I know a hostile question is about to be posed in a public lecture, for example, when a male questioner between the ages of 30 and 55 identifies himself as a pastor and explains that, while *he* was not disturbed by my positions, a lady in his congregation was very upset when she read.... Then comes a sequence of statements that so distort my views as to amount to parody. In that this sequence has frequently been repeated to me, I take it either that this woman is traveling all over America, or that there is a degree of coordination among reactionary critics. By their rhetoric ye shall know them...

Some of those who have left Christianity have done so in view of the behavior of Christians, others because their own convictions have changed. Professor Lüdemann belongs to the second category, along with Don Cupitt, whose *Taking Leave of God* preempted the question whether the author had left Christianity. This has permitted Cupitt, and I hope it will permit Lüdemann, to continue a vocation for theological thinking whose aim is reform.

My surprise peaks when Professor Lüdemann complains that the churches of Lower Saxony would like to close the door behind him now that he has left their fellowship of belief. The deliberation of his departure is plain, not only from his account, but in his own rhetoric. In the case of the resurrection, for example, he asserts as "fact that Jesus' body was not raised, but underwent natural decay." Various forms of belief in Jesus' life beyond the grave -- including Paul's in 1 Corinthians 15 — are compatible with the inference that his flesh rotted, but any such assertion is an inference, not a fact. Professor Lüdemann here assumes, however, that the resurrection is either material or nothing at all. That is a basis of his contention that Christianity's "points of reference, above all the resurrection of Jesus, have proved invalid."

Oddly, Lüdemann in this regard joins the vogue for a materialist view of the resurrection among many Evangelicals since the Enlightenment. He implicitly embraces their all-or-nothing insistence that if you do not believe Jesus was raised "in the same body" of flesh that was buried — despite Paul's explicit insistence to the contrary in 1 Corinthians 15:35-50 -- you are not really a Christian. In theological debate, as in conflict among nations, the clearer the caricature of the enemy, the greater the tendency to become like the enemy.

Once, during a meeting of the Jesus Seminar, a member ventured the opinion that the meeting was approaching an almost creedal formulation of some positions, all of them celebrated as anti-Fundamentalist. To this I replied that if anyone thought we had not been dealing with theology all along, he or she should wake up and smell the incense. Ten years later, ideological controversies within the Seminar in regard to staffing and which Fellows should be invited to speak are reminiscent of disputes within seminaries during periods of doctrinal dislocation. Excommunication in a variety of forms can be a tool not only of Catholic authorities and Evangelical colleges, but also of the secular institutions that object to them.

This reflex of secular Puritanism can be as trenchant as its fideistic counterparts. When Professor Lüdemann claims he knows as fact that Jesus was not raised from the dead and that belief in the resurrection is invalid, all the while complaining because the churches in his region do not like what he says, he approaches that trenchancy. Of course they objected — and I would agree from what he says that he has formulated his findings for the purpose of invalidating Christian faith, although my reading of the resurrection may be compared to his in some ways.

At various stages of a career, the development of a scholar's thought causes him or her to teach and research differently, and to be active among different constituencies. Recent progress in the study of religion has opened up a variety of institutional bases. Professor Lüdemann knows very well that his experience in North America offers models for education that differ from that of the theological faculty in Göttingen, as he shows in his objection to the place where he has been teaching:

> Only recently (1995), an oath dating from the year 1848 was reintroduced into my faculty after a lapse of some thirty years. Since then any newly appointed professor and any new lecturer must take the following oath: "I commit myself to presenting the theological disciplines honestly, clearly and thoroughly in agreement with the principles of the Evangelical Lutheran church." In my view, to tie theology to the church in this way goes against its claim to be a scientific, or even a truly academic discipline.

Given he cites Max Weber as an authority on what theology is, that finding is note surprising. He might well wish for a department of religion, where the issue of a confessional requirement would not arise and the emphasis would fall on the cultural side of inquiry. I would join him in that wish, and hope that his reassignment provides his university the incentive to establish such a department *alongside* its theological faculty. During the past few years, Professor Neusner and I have developed a model of advanced study in theology which is different again: the aim in this case is to permit students who are already trained in religion or theology to engage in comparative analysis of systems of belief and practice.

It would harm the study of religion if any of these models were to establish a monopoly in Germany, the United Kingdom, or North America. Institutions of confessional theology — in the form of theological faculties, divinity schools and seminaries — are indispensable for scholarship as well as for professional formation. They often develop levels of expertise and analytic foci that are not available elsewhere. They cannot be what they are if they pretend that requirements of faith and practice and devotion do not matter. Departments of religion scarcely need an *apologia* in these pages, but today they can justly claim that religious learning in a pluralistic age must itself be pluralistic if it is to avoid feeding the violence that threatens to consume us. Any university worth its salt should allow of dispute with regard to positions such as Professor Lüdemann's (although his strikes me as apologetically secular); pluralism in all disciplines — religion and theology included — should be part of the academy's approach. Whether the third model will move beyond experimental efforts remains to be seen, but my hope is that it will help cross-pollinate confessional theology and the critical study of religion. Comparison belongs among our analytic methods, provided it does not devolve into the summary claims alleging the unity of all religions that have given comparison a bad name in the past.

Meanwhile, of course, Professor Lüdemann wants to teach and research productively, and that is obviously in the University's interest. Many educators over the decades have called attention to the negative result of apartheid among the various faculties, institutes, programs, and schools within universities which, designed to develop competence by means of specificity, often precludes the discussion across disciplines that fosters genuine expertise. Finding Professor Lüdemann a home that supports his approach without limiting the range of his contacts is crucial to the range of disciplines, exegetical, historical, and theoretical, which make up the study of religion *and theology.*

Although that will prove a challenge to him as well as to his university, at least a university has the intellectual resources to address such questions. Spare a thought for scholars who are required to leave confessional institutions, not because they disagree globally with foundational beliefs of Christianity, but because they no longer believe as their colleagues do in modern doctrines such as biblical inerrancy or the biologically virgin birth or the Pauline authorship of Ephesians or the damnation of homosexuals. Think of the pastor-scholars within all religious traditions who, when the received form of the faith conflicts with their views, sometimes pay in pragmatic terms for the integrity of their perspectives: with their jobs.

Although the human cost of such separations can be high, it is also vital for the integrity and precision of our discipline. Confessional institutions press scholars to ask themselves what they believe and whether they believe, not only as a matter of voluntary reflection, but on a persistent basis and in the public domain. They are less likely to try, like Miguel de Unamuno's unbelieving priest (in *San Manuel Bueno, mártir*), to go through the motions of belief without faith. A hero for a certain kind of existentialism, Unamuno's character succeeded in educational terms only in infantalizing those he cared for. It would represent no progress for the critical study of religion to let all scholars off the hook of even posing the question of faith.

Everyone who reads about Jesus these days is bound to come across the hackneyed metaphor of scholars peering into a well and seeing their own reflections. Wells are in the first place for drawing water, and only occasionally for exercises in narcissism. When we look into the many sources of human religions (not just Jesus in the Gospels), we of course see ourselves, because they are powerful influences upon how we behave, feel, and think. That is why the study of religion, whether consciously confessional or not, inevitably involves the scholar's perspective within the curriculum of what is studied. Confessional theology makes that explicit, and we would be unwise to overlook that gift in our human concern for Professor Lüdemann and our enthusiasm for the cultural study of religion and comparative theology. Belief is obviously not the whole of religion, and yet remains a vital aspect of religion; if major institutions within of our discipline hold the act of belief up to public scrutiny, that benefits us all.

4

Hypocrisy and the New Testament

Philip R. Davies

University of Sheffield

Hypocrites! for you are as graves which cannot be seen, and the people who walk over them are not aware of them (Luke 11:44)

'Hypocrites': a favourite word in the mouth of Jesus, at least as the Synoptic evangelists represent him. In the case of Gerd Lüdemann, the issue that concerns me especially here is the state of the discipline of theology and of theologians. Lüdemann is only one of the victims in this.

There is no doubt in my mind, or in the mind, I would think, of any scholarly person outside the system itself, that the status of theology within German Universities is ambiguous (to put it gently). At one and the same time it functions within an institution of higher education and research that supports free enquiry as the basis for understanding; on the other hand, it serves and sustains a particular theory (Christian theology) as a prerequisite for such teaching and research, and its students are destined to take up professional positions within the Church.

Contradictions breed contradictions. Hence: if theology is an academic subject, what may a non-believer (or a believer in another religious system) expect to learn from teaching or research in a German faculty of theology? How may it contribute to her or his academic formation? That this 'academic' discipline operates within a confessional code and that without subscribing to that code one cannot be properly trained in the discipline? Seen in this way, theology has nothing to offer a University at all: it cannot educate properly those who do not accept its doctrinal premises. Theology *might* well have such a role, were it a critical discipline concerned with articulating, analyzing, comparing and critiquing the bases upon which theologies rest. But this is not the case in Germany; indeed, theology in this sense is virtually unknown anywhere in the world. We have to turn to the study of religion to find a properly academic discipline in this area. Yet theology and the study of religion are not the same, despite the efforts of many University departments in the UK, for example, to yoke the two together.

But this issue is not about institutions, nor disciplines. We are talking about individual people, people who vote, people who teach and research, who define the practice. I have no doubt that all of those responsible for Lüdemann's predicament regard themselves as scholars. Indeed, as Lüdemann himself points out, they are for the most part critical to the point of rejecting the notion of a parousia (and probably the resurrection: I remember the famous statement of the erstwhile Bishop of Durham, David Lewis, who called it 'juggling with bones'). And these scholars convey their academic heresies to their students. Good for them, we may say: they show that they are after all not doctrinally bound at all. There is room for critical thought here.

But not too much room, it seems. Most unresolved contradictions are lubricated by hypocrisy. The Church is aware that its future priests are being introduced to academic orthodoxies that deny what the Christian Church upholds as true doctrine. Yet the Church expects its priests to be academically trained (including a knowledge of Hebrew and Greek). This learning does not as a rule find its way into German pulpits (though I have heard one German sermon that explained the story of the Garden of Eden as a product of the 'Solomonic enlightenment' once beloved of Gerhard von Rad). Priests are quipped with knowledge that they cannot really pass on, even though they privately accept what they have ben taught. A church in which the leaders know what the flock do not is nevertheless not uncommon, but why should this situation be welcomed by the Church? I think the answer is apparent after a few moments of critical reflection. In the Gospels it is the Pharisees whom Jesus is made to attack as hypocrites. Scholarship knows this to be a rather biased portrait. But think for a moment: should the Church really be so hard on hypocrisy?

Yet it was not the hypocritical Church, but hypocritical scholars themselves who voted to expel Lüdemann from the Faculty. Let me surmise that their reasoning is this: his presence threatens the cosy compromise that wears a shroud of orthodoxy as well as a veneer of scholarship, the compromise that enables them to do critical research because they are supported by a rich intake of students who seek a sinecure in the Church. If this is indeed the reasoning, I can entirely accept its validity. Without the Church, can theology remain a major academic discipline? Can they bequeath their profession to a new generation? Where will the Church be without the prop of academi discourse to give it respectability? Is it not vital that faith and scholarship be yoked, for the good of both, and of course for the good of theology professors?

It would be a hard decision for most academic theologians to renounce the concordat of Church and University, destroy the tradition, endanger their own scholarship that thrives under a cosy collaboration. I find it hard to denounce too vehemently those who have voted not to rock the boat. Lüdemanns (there will be more of them) will destroy the system. Creating a truly critical theology, even if only in the person of one professor, may endanger an entire professional practice. Is continued hypocrisy so terrible? After all, the New Testament teaches that all humans sin and fall short. What better way to teach Christian doctrine than by illustrating this fundamental doctrine?

5

The End of a Great Tradition?

Robert W. Funk

The Weststar Institute

The opening paragraph of Albert Schweitzer's *Quest of the Historical Jesus* defines the character of German theology that has made it the model of Christian theology everywhere:

> When, at some future day, our period of civilisation shall lie, closed and completed, before the eyes of later generations, German theology will stand out as a great, a unique phenomenon in the mental and spiritual life of our time. . . . And the greatest achievement of German theology is the critical investigation of the life of Jesus. What it has accomplished here has laid down the conditions and determined the course of the religious thinking of the future.

Of course a great tradition does not perpetuate itself without constant vigilance and rigorous review. It appears that the great German tradition is in its death throes in the theological faculty at the University of Göttingen, a venue where it might have been expected to thrive.

The treatment of Professor Gerd Lüdemann by his theological colleagues may betray a terminal illness. An outstanding exponent of the best kind of German scholarship was David Friedrich Strauss. His remarkable *Life of Jesus Critically Examined* was published in two volumes in 1835 and 1836. Of Strauss' work Schweitzer wrote: "It is one of the most perfect things in the whole range of learned literature." Indeed, it is still in print after a century and a half in its scintillating English translation by George Eliot (Mary Ann Evans).

Strauss laid out much of the ground for the modern critical study of the gospels. He was able to do so not only because of his superior analytical and critical powers, but because he was emancipated from dogmatic commitments. The distinction of myth from history held no terrors for him. Strauss was honest in following the evidence as he conceived it to its ultimate conclusion. For that courage he stands as beacon for all subsequent generations.

The crux of the matter for Strauss was that he could no longer believe in a transcendent, personal God who intervenes supernaturally from time to time in the course of nature and history. His conviction was the result of the emergence of an acute historical consciousness, of the desire to know what really happened. It was also the consequence of the passing of the old worldview, the disappearance of the ancient mythical heavens. The defining moment of our times is the coincidence of the collapse of the mythical picture of the world with the divorce of the historical figure of Jesus from the early Christian mythological gospel.

A century after Strauss, Rudolf Bultmann, perhaps the greatest biblical scholar of the twentieth century, and another German scholar of deep conviction, argued that the primitive Christian gospel with its mythical framework had become untenable. We can no longer accept the ancient worldview in which the gospel is encased, he said, because it contradicts our reality sense, which after all is dictated by the modern worldview. If we are to continue proclaiming the Christian gospel, he concluded, we must "demythologize" it.

According to Bultmann, we can no longer accept the ancient cosmology that posited a heaven above as the abode of the gods and a hell beneath as the domain of Satan. We know that the earth is not the center of the galaxy, and we are no longer convinced that the universe was created simply for the benefit of human beings. We do not believe in spirits and demons that determine the fate of individuals. We no longer believe history will come to an abrupt end at the hands of an angry or vengeful God. We do not accept that death is punishment for sin; death is a part of the natural order. And we find incredible the monstrous notion that God would kill his own son in order to atone for the sins of humankind — propitiation by proxy, as it were. And we do not believe that the resurrection of Jesus involved the resuscitation of a corpse, which allegedly functioned as the doorway to another world and eternal life.

Now, a half century later, Gerd Lüdemann writes his letter to Jesus, in which he recapitulates most of what D. F. Strauss had written and Rudolf Bultmann had confessed. For the honesty and integrity inherent in the tradition of German academic theology, he is deprived of his post in the name of the tenets of "Evangelical Lutheran theology." It appears that the tradition of high scholarship represented by Strauss and Bultmann has died in the hands of the theological faculty at Göttingen.

Across the Atlantic, the Jesus Seminar is devoted to keeping the great German tradition alive. In addition to its own work on the history of Jesus, on the canon, on the history of the early Jesus movement, the Seminar has established the Order of D. F. Strauss. The Order is designed to honor the German pioneer, whose signal importance was little recognized in his own time, and to honor those who hold up the ideal of rigorous scientific theology. At its annual conference in October of 1999, the seventy-five scholars of the Seminar awarded the D. F. Strauss medal to Gerd Lüdemann for his pioneering work on the Jesus tradition. That work is summed up in his "Letter to Jesus," from which I now quote:

> So I prefer from now on to develop a purely human view of religion without having to legitimate myself by a higher authority which theologians call God. Through many discussions with colleagues about your [Jesus'] 'resurrection' and its correct interpretation I became painfully aware that these colleagues wanted to remain theologians at any price and secretly kept referring to another reality, without directly addressing it in the discussion of texts, stories or experiences. I can no longer accede to this secret presupposition.

It is for this fundamental honesty that your American colleagues are pleased to honor you as the true heir of D. F. Strauss and Rudolf Bultmann. We weep for the retreat into the principles of "Evangelical Lutheran theology" and the demise of the great German tradition at Göttingen.

6

Academic Freedom and the Plight of German Theological Studies

Douglas A. Knight

The period from 1968 through 1972 marked a turning point in the second half of the 20th century as social and intellectual upheavals spread throughout Europe and North America. I experienced it from the somewhat unusual vantage point of a foreigner in Germany engaged in graduate studies and confronted with impressive academic and cultural institutions with which I was not familiar. In October 1968 I arrived in Göttingen to begin doctoral studies in Old Testament at Georg-August-Universität. At the time, I knew little about this venerable institution other than its roster of distinguished biblical and other scholars since its founding in 1737. Even with my earlier studies in Oslo, I possessed little more than vague generalities about the German academic scene and did not have a clear sense of the distinctive relationship there among Church, state, and university. Upon completion of my degree program four years later, I returned to the United States a much different person—not only with the training and credentials needed for a career in teaching and research, but with a new understanding of political, cultural, ecclesiastical, as well as academic issues. As will be apparent in this essay, my "American" notions of church/state relations and academic freedom still persist, reinforced in line with the deep-seated challenges of the '60s and '70s. Considering matters now from the remove of three decades, I cannot help but think that those same cultural and institutional forces, particularly in their German form, set the stage for the conflict that subsequently engulfed my doctoral colleague in Göttingen of that period, Gerd Lüdemann.

At the base of the student unrest, both in Europe and in the U.S., was a fundamental questioning of authority—of governments over citizens, of the military-industrial establishment over political policies, of the First World over the Third

World, of one race over others, of males over females, of parents over children, of traditional social norms over the new generation's choices. No social institution was above the suspicion of those who became known as "the '60s generation" or—in German jargon, singling out the year of the beginning—"die Achtundsechziger." In Germany a special element was added: the parents and grandparents of the students were responsible for the greatest war and the most horrible, appalling massacre of modern times, likely of all times. As I observed in innumerable conversations and situations, the German students felt branded and fated: they were treated with suspicion and even hostility as they traveled in other countries; they often regarded their parents and their social institutions as being morally bankrupt; and they worried that the traits that characterized their predecessors may reside if not in their genes then in the cultural air they were breathing—the same atmosphere that could at once produce a Mozart and a Mengele, a Goethe and a Goebbels, a Dürer and a Führer. Much around them was to be discredited. Open criticism and intellectual honesty provided the best hope for escape from the cycle. Small wonder that 1969 brought the stunning loss of power by the Christian Democratic Party as the Social Democratic Party, in coalition with the Free Democrats, gained control of the government for the first time since the country's founding in 1949 and placed Willy Brandt in the chancellor's office. A popular student poster lampooned Franz-Josef Strauß, a leader of the opposition, by citing apocalyptic words attributed to him: "When the leveling of politics occurs, then will salvation descend out of the Bavarian mountains."

Education and religion, two phenomena pervading culture to its far reaches, came under special scrutiny, often in light of their roles during the Nazi period. Universities represent a crown of cultural achievement in Germany, as is the case in many other nations as well. Beginning in 1968, however, students challenged their strict structures of authority, demanding reform and practicing it even when it was not granted. They wanted membership on search committees and governing boards—*Drittelparität*, i.e. parity of professors, assistants (*Assistenten*, generally those who had completed their doctoral degrees and were working on the *Habilitation*), and students. They demanded the right to choose their examiners for their final comprehensive exams. They undermined conventional practices by not wearing black suits for their exams and by calling professors first by the title of "Mr." rather than "Herr Professor" (there were scarcely any women with full professorial status on German theology faculties at the time—a problem that is little changed today) and sometimes even by their first names. The leftist leanings of many students contributed to the inevitable conflicts that ensued, and theology students were not seldom among the leaders. The situation at Göttingen was not unlike that at most other German universities as the institution sought to contain the reform efforts. Individual faculty members often removed themselves from the fray, some refusing to examine students if the latter had a right to choose their examiners and others opting mainly to outlast that generation of students. Even though only minimal reforms seem to have survived to the present (and, of course, as in many countries those on the left have often moved toward the right as they advanced in age), the period of the '60s and '70s witnessed a direct, remarkable political engagement of students in their educational processes. It was for all of us there, even for those not actively involved, a heady, exhilarating time.

In comparison to education, however, religion was a mightier fortress to besiege for a variety of reasons: the ecclesiastical authorities operate from headquarters remote from the general populace; the Church is tangible mainly in its multitude of churches; the religion of the masses ranges from piety to apathy to atheism; and certain protections are guaranteed to religious bodies by the *Grundgesetz*, the "Basic Law" of the Federal Republic of Germany ratified in 1949. Following centuries of practice, "religion" in Germany meant at the time essentially the Christian "Church"— Evangelical (*Die Evangelische Kirche*, Lutheran, Reformed, or United) or Roman Catholic.[1] The Jewish presence was, as we know, decimated by the war. A minute proportion of the population belonged to other groups known as "sects" (e.g., Methodists, Baptists, Pentecostals, Eastern Orthodox). Some 93% of the entire German population in 1970 were nominally members of the main Christian groups—nominally in the sense that, though the overwhelming majority scarcely attended church services except for baptisms, weddings, and funerals, they had not taken the step of presenting themselves at government offices and formally withdrawing their membership. The late '60s, however, saw the beginning of a deliberate decline of Church membership as an increasing number joined the ranks of the *Konfessionslose*, while at the same time expanding immigration precipitated an upsurge of the non-Christian population as well. For all the force of the confrontation thirty years ago, the demographic context today in which Lüdemann has been judged is quite different. The year 1968 presented a situation in which virtually the entire population seemed on the surface to be homogeneously Christian. Today with the addition of the former East German territory, however, only two-thirds of the German population belong to the two large Christian Churches, the rest being adherents of other faiths (some 4% Muslims, over 1% Orthodox Christian, a similar fraction belonging to a wide range of other religious communities) or of none at all.[2] The Göttingen faculty's repudiation of Lüdemann occurs, in other words, in the face of a much less Christian, more heterogeneous religious and non-religious population than had previously existed within the country.

During my doctoral studies I was informed of a distinction that I still fail to comprehend, not in terms of the German law but in terms of its pragmatic effects:

---

[1] The capitalized word "Church" in this discussion designates the officially recognized Christian denominations in Germany, which can vary from province to province.
[2] Statistics derive from the November 2001 report of the Religionswissenschaftlicher Medien- und Informationsdienst e. V.

that Germany does not have a *Staatskirche*[3] but a *Volkskirche*, not a state Church but a people's Church. According to this notion, the state guarantees religious freedom (Article 4) and permits the formation of religious associations as corporations under public law (also included in the excerpt in Article 140). At the same time, however, the state fosters the religion of the majority in each province: it grants the religious associations the right to conduct religious education as a standard part of the curriculum in public schools (except for non-denominational schools) (Article 7);[4] it protects Sunday and certain other holidays as "Tage der Arbeitsruhe und der seelischen Erhebung" (days of rest from work and of spiritual improvement; Article 140); and it empowers religious associations to levy taxes on the basis of civil tax lists (Article 140). The last element is hardly insignificant, for without it the Church would likely have inadequate means to maintain itself, given the sparse involvement of the people in the life of the Church. The state does not tax the people for the Church—so goes the argument—but rather only "collects" for the Church the tax levied by the Church on its members.[5] Despite the repeated explanations of German colleagues, to my American mind this distinction struck and still strikes me as specious. The Church has a vested interest in preserving this cozy arrangement with the state, and it protested vociferously and successfully when, during an election campaign in the '70s, the Free Democratic Party proposed an end to the state's collection of the *Kirchensteuer*. Of course, if the difference between a *Staatskirche* and a *Volkskirche* signifies primarily a separation significant enough to allow the Church to criticize state policies, then the dominant German Churches can demonstrate an important record in post-War politics, often even more pointed dissent than is seen on the U.S. religious scene. But the connective tissue between the German Church and state, including their contractual arrangements, is not severed.

The Church-tax was not the only object in the criticism of religion three decades ago. One heard a deriding of the "theology of stones," i.e. too much of the Church's budget going toward the expensive maintenance of its old, albeit historic edifices. Even though a portion of the cost of the country's social programs stemmed

---

[3] The *Grundgesetz* states explicitly in Article 140 (a section extracted from the Weimar Constitution of 11 August 1919): "Es besteht keine Staatskirche" (There shall be no state church).

[4] As my family and I discovered in 1987-88 during a sabbatical leave in Tübingen, many of the lower schools by then offered students a choice between a course in religion or one in ethics.

[5] In the year 2000 the taxes collected for the Church totaled ca. DM 17 billion (ca. US$ 7.5 billion), almost evenly divided between the Evangelical and Roman Catholic Churches. The tax is withheld directly from a person's wages together with the regular state taxes. Members of the many smaller denominations or religions can now also file for their "church-tax" to benefit their own religious associations. This latter change is only one of the reforms sought in court by the "sects" that wish to enjoy rights similar to those of the two large Churches.

from the Church's income, this fact did not mitigate the criticisms of the power and costs of the Church hierarchy or the questions about the clergy's job security and state-recognized standing. And most immediately in the minds of many was the Church's substantial silence and at times even outright complicity, despite important voices of protest, as the nation waged two World Wars: if the Church had absolutely condemned, with all of its force opposed, and from every pulpit railed against the militarism and the ideology behind it, the outcome would surely have been different. The 1968 publication of the tendentious but much noted book by Joachim Kahl, *Das Elend des Christentums: oder, Plädoyer für eine Humanität ohne Gott* (its English title: *The Misery of Christianity: or, A Plea for a Humanity without God*),[6] which stridently sketched a centuries-long history of reprehensible acts carried out in the name of Christianity and called for a full separation of state from Church, elicited expressions of acclamation from one side and condemnation from the other.

The content of Lüdemann's case derives only indirectly from the criticisms and reform efforts of the '60s and '70s, but the lines of conflict are directly related, in my view. The collision course was paved by the very tradition and laws that support the study of theology in the universities as well as the state-sanctioned religious instruction in lower schools as well. The theology departments in universities are explicitly and legally tied by confession to either the Evangelical Church or the Roman Catholic Church; several universities (Tübingen, Munich, Frankfort, Bochum, and Münster) have two separate departments, one connected to each Church. As such, these departments are essentially extensions of the respective Churches, and it is expected that any graduate of the department should be able to hold an office in the Church. I must admit to being shocked when, upon pressing the question, I discovered that a Jew would not be granted a degree from the theology faculties, nor would a Buddhist or Hindu or other religious adherent. Individual faculty members, as well as the graduates, are expected to be advocates of the Church that provides the instruction in each theology department, but explicitly what they should or should not advocate is unclear until an ad hoc judgment is announced. Furthermore, the orthodox line is determined by the Church hierarchy, not by the few in the pew nor by the majority of the Church-tax payers. And therein lies the rub. This situation is not unique to Göttingen. What happened to Lüdemann could well have occurred in any German university with a theology department, to my knowledge; he is by far not the only theology faculty member to have been repudiated by the Evangelical Church or the Roman Catholic Church in post-War Germany.

The educational system in the United States is quite the opposite in this respect. In a state university a department of religion must by law refrain from confessional advocacy, which is permitted only in private institutions. Although

---

[6] German original, Reinbek bei Hamburg: Rowohlt, 1968 (revised and expanded edition, 1993); English translation, Harmondsworth: Penguin, 1971.

non-Germans are often not aware of it, the theology departments of German universities are more similar to denominational universities and seminaries in the United States than they are to the religion departments in American non-denominational and state universities.[7] Or stated in terms of the long-used dichotomy between "theological studies" and "religious studies,"[8] the German universities provide programs of theological studies much more so than they do curricula of religious studies.[9] Somewhat ironically, they may include instruction about other religions of the world and allow German students and faculty to study or teach in other religious environments, without reciprocally welcoming or even permitting other religious adherents to function equally in the German theology departments. The alternative is for instruction on other religions, including Judaism, to be offered in other departments of the university than in the theology department. "Theology" in this sense equates to Christian theology; the system precludes any non-Christian religion from having a "theology." In 1882 Julius Wellhausen changed departments when he decided he was not suited to continue teaching those who would become Christian ministers. Lüdemann was also encouraged to resign from the Theologische Fakultät in Göttingen and to relocate to the Philosophische Fakultät.[10] Quite aside from the fact that this option was not open to him by vote of the latter faculty, he maintains resolutely that theological studies should be possible in the university without a requirement for confessional allegiance. The legal conditions governing the controversy are surely much more complex than a casual reader of the *Grundgesetz* can suspect, but on the face of it the fundamental rights would appear to be in Lüdemann's favor: freedom of religious expression and practice (Articles 4), protection against discrimination on grounds of religion (Article 3), prohibition of censure (Article 5), and guarantee of state appointments regardless of religious belief (Article 140, from Article 136 of the Weimar Constitution).

---

[7] The situation may vary in structure or effect in other European countries as well as in other nations of the world. My comments here focus on the German situation in comparison with that in the United States.

[8] For recent discussions of this distinction, which dates at least to the '60s, see Conrad Cherry, *Hurrying toward Zion: Universities, Divinity Schools, and American Protestantism* (Bloomington and Indianapolis: Indiana University, 1995) 112-23; Walter H. Capps, *Religious Studies: The Making of a Discipline* (Minneapolis: Fortress, 1995) 331-48; and Peter C. Hodgson, *God's Wisdom: Toward a Theology of Education* (Louisville: Westminster John Knox, 1999) 125-40.

[9] Against this background, I requested in 1986 that my professorial position at Vanderbilt University Divinity School be designated as Hebrew Bible rather than Old Testament, as it had been previously. Despite certain inadequacies associated with the term "Hebrew Bible," for me it represents an effort to move beyond the confessional confines of the term "Old Testament."

[10] The "Philosophische Fakultät" in German universities embraces most areas of the humanities, not solely the field of philosophy.

The issue reduces to the problem of academic freedom. Thus is how we in the higher education system of the United States, at least, would be inclined to view it. I was told explicitly by a German theology professor that full "academic freedom" does not exist in the context of German theology departments. Another informed me that it is an institutional issue, not an intellectual concern, insofar as there is a contractual agreement between Church and state to provide theological instruction at the universities. There is, apparently, no place for the fundamental, extreme application of the critical principle if it challenges or threatens the institutional and confessional cause. One must, in other words, stop short of the ultimate criticism—or switch to a different setting to express it. Academic freedom exists, however, precisely for the purpose of affording protection to those who, while conducting their work responsibly, challenge basic political, institutional, or intellectual positions. Such work is above all needed in our current global, postmodern, postcolonial age. Not offering this protection of thought can imply, in fact, that an institution fears itself to be vulnerable and its positions assailable. Yet ideas need to be presented in the open, without fear of repercussions and with the expectation that the discussion will ultimately issue in new clarity and understanding.

For over two centuries now German academics have pioneered in the study of religion and theology, not the least in my own fields of biblical and ancient Near Eastern studies. This tradition of scholarship, with its impressive array of break-through insights and painstaking contributions, still belongs to the working stock of much of our current research, even where it is presented as a counterpoint. I must admit, however, that the Lüdemann-case has cast the German scholarly legacy in a different light for me. While considerable latitude obviously prevailed as scholars in this tradition introduced many of the critical methods driving the discipline until the middle of the 20th century, it is now more than ever apparent that service to the Church always functioned as a constraint. Scholarship crosses international borders, and it is important to understand under what terms and with what restraints it is being conducted in each context. A cloud now hangs unavoidably over the great heritage of German theological scholarship that many of us have regarded as our forerunner. To me personally this realization comes with no little sadness. While most of us who engage in the study of religion are inheritors of the German scholarship of the past, I am also personally and profoundly in debt to the place that welcomed me warmly and provided me with deep friendships, cultural and political awareness, and professional training.

These reflections on the nature of German theological scholarship in light of the Lüdemann-case bring to mind an earlier exchange. In 1899 Wellhausen[11]

---

[11] Wellhausen, "Zur apokalyptischen Literatur," *Skizzen und Vorarbeiten*, vol. 6 (Berlin: Georg Reimer, 1899) 225-34.

criticized Hermann Gunkel sharply for applying the new religion-historical method in *Schöpfung und Chaos.*[12] Gunkel responded with disappointment: "We recognize this voice very well, but we are astonished to hear it coming from so far-sighted a man whom we have honored as our pioneer and leader."[13]

---

[12] Gunkel, *Schöpfung und Chaos in Urzeit und Endzeit: Eine religionsgeschichtliche Untersuchung über Gen 1 und Ap Joh 12* (Göttingen: Vandenhoeck & Ruprecht, 1895).

[13] Gunkel, "Aus Wellhausen's neuesten apokalyptischen Forschungen: Einige principielle Erörterungen," *Zeitschrift für wissenschaftliche Theologie* 42 (1899) 611.

7

Academic Theology in Germany

Reinhard G. Kratz

The Dean of the Theological Faculty of the Georg-August-University Göttingen

1

Theological faculties in Germany are State institutions, guaranteed by agreements between the autonomous Protestant regional churches (Landeskirchen) or the Roman Catholic Church and the State. Theology is one of the disciplines taught at the German State or public universities, which the State provides for the education and professional training of its citizens; in this context of the university, mutual exchange between theology and other disciplines is being promoted.

At the same time, the theological faculties in Germany also have a function for the Church. On the one hand, through their academic research and teaching, they contribute to the development and growth of Christian knowledge. On the other hand, they provide the academic training for the future clergy and teachers of religious instruction (at German schools).

Thus, theological faculties in Germany hold a dual legal status. This dual status reflects the interest of both the State and the Church. In conformity with German and European academic tradition the theological faculties at State universities are established according to and protected by the constitutional right of freedom of religion. Their State status protects them from patronizing by the Church, their Church status from encroachments of the State. The dual status guarantees the unrestricted freedom of teaching and research at the theological faculties and for all their members, as long as they keep to the laws and constitution – a fact that applies to all State institutions.

As a consequence of the dual status of theological faculties their professors have a special standing in regard to their regulations of employment. They are appointed (as a rule) into a tenured position, which demands loyalty towards the State and its laws, in particular those that regulate the relationship of State and Church. At the same time, through their research in the field of theology and Christian knowledge and through their training of the future clergy and teachers of religion, they are required to serve church interests, with a corresponding demand for loyalty within, the rights and duties resulting from the State-Church contract.

Because of this express duty to the Church, the position which a professor at a theological faculty holds is called a "konfessionsgebundenes Staatsamt", i.e. his or her appointment depends, in addition to the ordinary prerequisites for a professorship, on his or her belonging to the very church to which the faculty is affiliated. This has its foundation in the right of religious freedom which is guaranteed by the Constitution; it is the Constitution which grants that the teaching and training of the future clergy at the State University is only the church's concern, thus protecting the religious autonomy of the church. Academic theology as taught at theological faculties at State universities, including biblical and dogmatic criticism, is understood by the churches to belong to what concerns them. Therefore the denominational prerequisite is not in contradiction to, but in agreement with, the freedom of teaching and research.

2

At the theological faculties in Germany, the professors who are teaching and researching there and the students who are studying there, generally belong to the denomination of their faculty. The degrees (Diplom, Magister, Promotion, Habilitation), insofar as they are theological degrees, are linked to the confessional status of the faculty, either Protestant (including all member churches in the Ecumenical Council of Churches) or Roman Catholic. In addition, persons of other denominations or religions are free to study, teach and do research at theological faculties in Germany, because teaching and research is freely accessible to all and not bound by religious denomination. Such persons, however, cannot hold denominationally bound public positions or take exams for a denominationally bound theological degree (as above). Professors belonging to other Christian churches or non-Christian religions are welcome according to the same rules and conditions as are professors of other – non-theological – faculties: theological faculties can invite them as guest professors or appoint them under special status, including full and unrestricted academic freedom. Students of other churches are welcome, as are students from other faculties or non-theological study programs who want to study one of the theological disciplines or do a course-program in religious studies without the goal of acquiring a theological degree. There exists a long-standing interdisciplinary co-operation between the theological and the philosophical faculty (i.e. the humanities department). Examinations are held by professors of the theological faculty together with professors of the philosophical faculty according to the regulations of the philosophical faculty.

If we look at the history of academic theology, especially the historical criticism of the Bible, it becomes obvious that most of its basic and often quite revolutionary research and resulting schools of research – e.g. Pentateuch criticism, New Testament criticism or the History of Religions School – were and are found at denominationally bound theological faculties. The churches often viewed this research and these schools with scepticism or even disapproval, but they have – at least as far as the Protestant churches are concerned - never actually stopped or suppressed them; sometimes they have welcomed and encouraged them. Today historical biblical criticism and criticism of theology and the teachings of the church form an undisputed part of the academic study course for the future clergy and teachers of religion, and their contribution to our understanding of the church is widely acknowledged. The dual status of the theological faculties in Germany thus functions as a guarantor of freedom in research and teaching. Here can be seen in what way a tolerant and liberal relationship between State and Church does not prevent, but rather allows a free academic theology.

3

According to the statement by the Collegium of the Theological Faculty of 22 April 1998 – as already noted on the invitation to that meeting of 15 April – and a further statement by the then Dean (Professor Eberhard Busch) of 22 December 1998, to the same result, Professor Lüdemann has assumed a position "in striking contradiction to the definition and the purpose of a theological faculty".

With this statement, the Theological Faculty does not at all refer to the results of Professor Lüdemann's research, undertaken and published by him as professor and member of a denominationally bound theological faculty – a research with results which in fact have been a matter of debate in denominationally bound theological faculties for the last 100 years.

Nor does the Theological Faculty refer, with this statement, to the "personal decision", which Professor Lüdemann felt called to make years after joining the Theological Faculty. The Collegium has explicitly stated its "respect" for this decision growing out of the critical research of the New Testament of the last 100 years and Professor Lüdemann's own recent insights into this research. A conflict of personal faith and critical biblical study is not anything unusual. Where it arises, it usually occurs during the first years of studies, and mostly with students from a pietistic background, who then soon begin to understand that it is not history that generates faith, but faith that makes history. — A point, one might certainly debate.

Rather, with its statement the Collegium refers exclusively to declarations made by Professor Lüdemann regarding his duties and his position as professor at a theological faculty at a State university – in a denominationally bound state tenure ("konfessionsgebundenes Staatsamt") which he cannot (any longer) settle with his conscience. He has declared the education and training of the future clergy and religious teachers, as it is provided by German universities, according to our laws and based on the Christian creeds, to be a mere hypocrisy. Furthermore he has declared that theology as taught at theological faculties in Germany does not stand up to academic standards. Because of these convictions, Professor Lüdemann has publicly and explicitly renounced Christianity, thus leaving the very basis on which the theological faculties are founded (according to the well-considered tenets of our Constitution) and on which he as well as his colleagues have been teaching and doing research over the past years with absolute academic freedom and without any church interference. He is, of course, free to act as his conscience bids him to do. At the same time, one would expect the logical conclusion of his leaving the church and resigning from his position as a member of the theological faculty – in accordance with the best tradition of free Protestant theology.

This, and only this is the reason why the Theological Faculty has, on 19 November 1998, asked the President of the University, that a position be made available for Professor Lüdemann that is in agreement with his conscience and his convictions, while maintaining all his rights and duties of a German university professor. It is no more than consistent with Professor Lüdemann's renunciation of Christianity and it follows from the legal Church-State agreement that this position has to be "outside of the study program for the future clergy"; this new position automatically frees him from Church connected obligations. The change of his chair into one for "History and Literature of Early Christianity", with his formerly held chair in New Testament being open for replacement, is no more than the logical result. The logical location for this chair for "History and Literature of Early Christianity" held by a professor who does not want to be affiliated with the Church and its confession, would be within the philosophical faculty (humanities department). Since the Göttingen philosophical faculty, however, has declined to accept Professor Lüdemann as a member, he has to stay in the theological faculty, where he is accorded a special status with all the rights and duties except those, which he himself has denounced and rejected.

He is free and unimpeded in his teaching and research, as he sees it. His lectures and seminars are open for everyone, both for students of theology and for students of other study programs or faculties. It is an honoured tradition for German students to take courses outside of their own academic field, where they are perceived to be of relevance and interest to them. Professor Lüdemann has the unrestricted right to hold examinations in his field of "History and Literature of the Early Christianity"; however, he cannot hold examinations within the study program of Protestant Theology (pastors and teachers) as that is based on the very laws, which he has rejected as a matter of conscience. The financial endowment of his chair corresponds to that of the others, in certain respects it is even better. Additional funding for the chair, as it is often granted in conjunction with a new appointment, does not extend beyond the usual period of five years. This holds for Professor Lüdemann as much as for the rest of his colleagues. His personal income, as with all professors being a State salary, is guaranteed.

This settlement, which was stipulated by the President of the University after consultation with the Theological Faculty of the University in Göttingen and which was confirmed by the Minister for Science and Culture of the State of Lower Saxony in agreement with the Confederation of Evangelical Churches in Lower Saxony, was originally accepted and agreed by Professor Lüdemann. Why he has now turned to publicly reject it and is seeking to reverse it in court, he alone knows.

Wissenschaftliche Theologie in Deutschland

Reinhard G. Kratz

Der Dekan
der Theologischen Fakultät
der Georg-August-Universität in Göttingen

1

Theologische Fakultäten in Deutschland sind staatliche Einrichtungen. Der Staat hat sich selbst verpflichtet, die Theologie als Teil der Wissenschaften in seinen Universitäten zu verankern und den gegenseitigen Austausch mit anderen Wissenschaften zu fördern.

Zugleich erfüllen die Theologischen Fakultäten in Deutschland eine kirchliche Aufgabe. Zum einen tragen sie durch ihre wissenschaftliche Tätigkeit zur Entfaltung der kirchlichen Lehre bei. Zum anderen sorgen sie für die wissenschaftliche Ausbildung der künftigen Geistlichen und Religionslehrer.

Die Theologischen Fakultäten in Deutschland besitzen somit juristisch einen Doppelstatus. Dieser Doppelstatus liegt im Interesse sowohl des Staates als auch der Kirche. In Übereinstimmung mit der deutschen und der europäischen Wissenschaftstradition sind die Theologischen Fakultäten an staatlichen Universitäten angesiedelt und stehen unter dem Schutz des Grundrechts der Religionsfreiheit. Der staatliche Status schützt vor Bevormundungen durch die Kirche, der kirchliche vor Übergriffen des Staates. Der Doppelstatus begründet die uneingeschränkte Freiheit in Lehre und Forschung an den Theologischen Fakultäten, sofern sich ihre Mitglieder, was für alle staatlichen Institutionen gilt, sich auf dem Boden der geltenden Gesetze bewegen.

Aus dem Doppelstatus der Theologischen Fakultäten resultiert eine besondere dienstrechtliche Stellung ihrer Professoren. Sie werden (in der Regel) in ein Beamtenverhältnis auf Lebenszeit berufen und sind daher dem Staat und seinen Gesetzen, insbesondere solchen, die das Verhältnis von Staat und Kirche in Deutschland regeln, verpflichtet. Zugleich erfüllen sie mit der wissenschaftlichen Entfaltung der kirchlichen Lehre und mit der Ausbildung von Geistlichen und Religionslehrern eine kirchliche Aufgabe und sind damit der Kirche und ihren vom Staat gewährten, vertraglich geregelten Rechten verpflichtet. Mit Rücksicht auf diese kirchliche Aufgabe ist ihr Amt als sogenanntes konfessionsgebundenes Staatsamt ausgestaltet, d.h. die Verleihung des Amtes ist über die allgemeinen Berufsvoraussetzungen hinaus davon abhängig, dass ein Professor der Konfession angehört, der die Fakultät zugeordnet ist. Die Konfessionsbindung trägt dem Umstand Rechnung, dass die Verfassung die kirchlichen Aufgaben eines Theologieprofessors – im Rahmen der staatlichen Universität – als eigene Angelegenheit der Kirchen und Teil ihrer freien Religionsausübung schützt. Und indem die Kirchen die wissenschaftliche Theologie, einschließlich der Bibel- und Dogmenkritik, im Rahmen von staatlichen Theologischen Fakultäten als ihre eigene Angelegenheit betrachten, steht die Konfessionsbindung nicht im Widerspruch, sondern in Einklang mit der Freiheit von Lehre und Forschung.

2

An den Theologischen Fakultäten in Deutschland lehren und forschen daher in erster Linie Professoren und studieren in erster Linie Studenten derjenigen Konfession, der die Fakultät zugeordnet ist. Auch die Abschlüsse (Diplom, Magister, Promotion, Habilitation) sind, sofern es sich um theologische Abschlüsse handelt, konfessionsgebunden, entweder protestantisch (einschließlich aller im Ökumenischen Rat der Kirchen vertretenen Denominationen) oder römisch-katholisch.

Darüber hinaus forschen, lehren und studieren an den Theologischen Fakultäten in Deutschland auch Personen anderer Konfessionen oder Religionen, da Forschung und Lehre uneingeschränkt frei und nicht konfessionsgebunden sind. Nur können solche Personen keine konfessionsgebundenen Staatsämter bekleiden und keine theologischen Examina ablegen. Für Professoren anderer christlicher oder nichtchristlicher Konfessionen gilt dieselbe Regelung wie für Professoren anderer, nichttheologischer Fakultäten: Sie können als Gastprofessoren auf Zeit eingeladen oder in einem Sonderstatus an Theologischen Fakultäten installiert werden und genießen hier uneingeschränkte Freiheit in Forschung und Lehre in ihrem Fachgebiet. Für Studierende anderer Konfessionen gilt dieselbe Regelung wie für Studierende anderer, nichttheologischer Studiengänge, die eines der theologischen Fächer oder allgemeine Religionswissenschaft studieren, aber keinen theologischen Abschluss anstreben: Für sie besteht eine längst eingespielte, enge interdisziplinäre Kooperation zwischen der Theologischen und der Philosophischen Fakultät. Die Examina werden von Theologieprofessoren gemeinsam mit Professoren der Philosophischen Fakultät nach der Ordnung der Philosophischen Fakultät abgenommen.

Die Geschichte der theologischen Wissenschaften, insbesondere der historisch-kritischen Bibelwissenschaften, lehrt, dass nicht wenige ihrer grundlegenden, teilweise umstürzenden Erkenntnisse oder Richtungen – z.B. die Pentateuchkritik, die Evangelienkritik oder die Religionsgeschichtliche Schule – im Rahmen von konfessionsgebundenen Theologischen Fakultäten entstanden sind. Die Kirchen standen diesen Erkenntnissen oder Richtungen oft skeptisch oder auch ablehnend gegenüber, haben sie aber – jedenfalls im protestantischen Raum – nie verhindert, zuweilen auch begrüßt und gefördert. Heute ist es längst eine Selbstverständlichkeit, dass auch und gerade die historische Bibel- und Dogmenkritik das ihre zur wissenschaftlichen Ausbildung der Geistlichen und Religionslehrer sowie zur Entfaltung der kirchlichen Lehre beiträgt. Der Doppelstatus der Theologischen Fakultäten hat sich in Deutschland somit als Garant der Freiheit von Forschung und Lehre bewährt. Er ist ein Zeichen der Liberalität im Verhältnis von Staat und Kirche zur Ermöglichung und ungehinderten Entfaltung einer freien wissenschaftlichen Theologie.

3

Wie die – bereits in der Einladung vom 15. April 1998 angekündigte – Erklärung des Collegiums der Theologischen Fakultät vom 22. April 1998 feststellt und die Erklärung des damaligen Dekans (Prof. Eberhard Busch) vom 22. Dezember1998 sinngemäß wiederholt, hat sich Professor Lüdemann "in einen eklatanten Widerspruch zu Charakter und Aufgabe einer Theologischen Fakultät begeben".

Diese Feststellung beruht nicht im geringsten auf den Ergebnissen seiner Forschungen, die er im konfessionsgebundenen Staatsamt und als Mitglied einer konfessionsgebundenen Theologischen Fakultät erzielt und publiziert hat und die im übrigen schon seit über 100 Jahren in konfessionsgebundenen Theologischen Fakultäten diskutiert werden.

Die Feststellung beruht auch nicht auf den "persönlichen Entscheidungen", die Professor Lüdemann lange nach seinem Eintritt in die Theologische Fakultät aufgrund der über 100jährigen kritischen Erforschung des Neuen Testaments und seiner eigenen wissenschaftlichen Einsichten neuerdings für sich treffen zu müssen glaubt und die das Collegium ausdrücklich "respektiert". Der Konflikt von persönlichem Glauben und kritischer Bibelwissenschaft ist nichts Ungewöhnliches. Er tritt meist schon im Studium und bevorzugt bei Studenten mit pietistischem Hintergrund auf, die allerdings bald begreifen, dass nicht die Geschichte den Glauben, sondern der Glaube Geschichte macht. Auch darüber lässt sich reden.

Die Feststellung des Collegiums bezieht sich ausschließlich auf Äußerungen von Professor Lüdemann, die seine dienstlichen Verpflichtungen sowie seine dienstrechtliche Stellung in einem konfessionsgebundenen Staatsamt betreffen. Da er beides mit seinem Gewissen nicht (mehr) vereinbaren kann, die nach dem Willen des Gesetzes praktizierte Ausbildung von Geistlichen und Religionslehrern auf dem Boden des christlichen Bekenntnisses vielmehr als Heuchelei bezeichnet und der wissenschaftlichen Theologie an den Theologischen Fakultäten die Wissenschaftlichkeit abspricht, hat er sich öffentlich und ausdrücklich vom Christentum losgesagt und damit selbst die Basis verlassen, auf der er wie alle anderen Professoren seiner Fakultät lange Jahre in aller Freiheit und ganz ohne kirchliche Einmischung geforscht und gelehrt hat und auf der die Theologischen Fakultäten (aus den von den Vätern der Verfassung wohlerwogenen Gründen) nun einmal ruhen. Auch das steht ihm vollkommen frei, nur sollte man erwarten, dass er dann auch die Konsequenzen zieht, aus der Kirche austritt und die Theologische Fakultät verlässt, wie es sich nach bester Tradition der freien protestantischen Theologie gehörte.

Darum, und nur darum, hat die Theologische Fakultät von sich aus am 19. November 1998 den Präsidenten der Universität ersucht, Professor Lüdemann – unter Wahrung aller Rechte und Pflichten eines deutschen Universitätsprofessors – in einen Status zu versetzen, den er mit seinem Gewissen vereinbaren kann. Dass dieser Status "außerhalb der Studiengänge des Theologischen Nachwuchses" zu suchen ist, versteht sich nach der Lossagung Professor Lüdemanns vom Christentum aufgrund der geltenden Rechtslage von selbst und befreit ihn von der Wahrnehmung der mit seinem Amt verbundenen, ungeliebten kirchlichen Aufgabe. Die Umwidmung seines Lehrstuhls in eine Professur für "Geschichte und Literatur des frühen Christentums" und die Einrichtung einer Ersatzprofessur für "Neues Testament" ist die logische Folge. Da die Philosophische Fakultät, der natürliche Ort für jemanden, der kein konfessionsgebundenes Staatsamt innehaben möchte, keine Verwendung für ihn hat, muss Professor Lüdemann an der Theologischen Fakultät verbleiben, allerdings in einem Sonderstatus, der ihm alles erlaubt und nichts nimmt, was er nicht schon selbst von sich gewiesen hätte.

Er kann weiterhin ungehindert forschen und lehren, was er für richtig hält. Seine Veranstaltungen sind für jedermann zugänglich, und zwar für Studenten der Theologie ebenso wie für Studenten anderer Studiengänge. In Deutschland besuchen Studenten gerne und fleißig Lehrveranstaltungen außerhalb ihres eigenen Studienfaches, sofern diese von Belang und Interesse sind. Professor Lüdemann hat uneingeschränktes Prüfungsrecht an der Universität für sein Fachgebiet "Geschichte und Literatur des frühen Christentums", nur nicht im Studiengang Evangelische Theologie (Pfarramt und Lehramt), dessen gesetzliche Grundlagen zu akzeptieren er sich außer Stande sieht. Seine Berufungszusagen galten für ihn wie für alle Professoren befristet auf fünf Jahre. Die gegenwärtige finanzielle Ausstattung seines Lehrstuhls bewegt sich im üblichen Rahmen, in mancher Hinsicht sogar darüber hinaus. Sein dienstrechtlicher Status als Professor bleibt unangetastet, sein persönliches Einkommen ist wie bisher gesichert.

Mit der Regelung, die der Präsident der Universität im Einvernehmen mit der Theologischen Fakultät in Göttingen vorgeschlagen und der zuständige Minister für Wissenschaft und Kultur des Landes Niedersachsen im Einvernehmen mit der Konföderation Evangelischer Kirchen in Niedersachsen vollzogen hat und die mittlerweile von zwei unabhängigen deutschen Gerichten bestätigt wurde, hatte sich Professor Lüdemann zunächst einverstanden erklärt. Warum er nun öffentlich und gerichtlich dagegen zu Felde zieht, weiß nur er allein.

8

Bernhard Lang

University of Paderborn, Germany
University of St. Andrews, Scotland

The Lüdemann case reveals the strange situation of the German university departments of theology. They are, in terms of Mary Douglas's Purity and Danger, "matter out of place" and therefore impure. They belong neither fully to the state-funded university with its tradition and guarantee of academic freedom of research and teaching, nor do they form part of the structure of the Protestant (or, in the case of Catholic theology departments, of the Catholic) church. Their status is defined, both by the German constitution and by contracts concluded between state and church, as academic institutions for the professional training of clergy and of school teachers of religion (i.e., either Catholic or Protestant doctrine) under ecclesiastical supervision.

The state supplies office space, lecture rooms, funds for libraries and research, employs professors, research and teaching assistants, and secretaries; the church grants and, in the case of doctrinal or moral dissent, withdraws the professor's teaching license. This system works efficiently as long as professors subscribe to doctrines and hold views currently favored by bishops, church presidents, or ecclesiastical boards. As soon as a professor is felt to depart from such doctrines and views, he is in trouble. If someone readily admits his or her errors and recants heretical views, the license to teach is no longer endangered. In case of a professor's refusal, however, the church withdraws the ecclesiastical license to teach and demands of the state to employ someone else, i.e. someone whose teaching is, from the ecclesiastical perspective, unobjectionable.

Bound by the constitution and rules set up by contract, the state — usually represented by the minister of academic affairs — follows the directions given by the church. At the same time, the state usually protects the incriminated professor's academic freedom by leaving him on the payroll and by associating him with some other university department (e.g. the department of philosophy). A relocation to a department of religious studies is not generally possible, because most universities lack such a department. In some German universities, religious studies forms a sub-discipline within theology and is therefore supervised by the church.

It would be wrong to assume that this situation is unbearable only for professors such as Gerd Lüdemann, for intellectuals who are critical of traditional ecclesiastical doctrine or authority. As a matter of fact, this situation has done, and continues to do, much harm in many other and more subtle ways, for it fosters academic mediocrity and serves to keep truly critical and creative spirits out of the discipline.

As a result, academic theology in Germany has become a rather dull, uninspiring discipline. It neither attracts gifted students nor commands much respect among colleagues teaching in non-theological disciplines. As a further result, the representatives of non-theological disciplines rarely rely on the results of research done within departments of divinity; instead, they study the writings of the great theologians, the church's social teaching, and Christian mentalities themselves — with more freedom and generally with better results. It has become difficult even for established theologians to compete with other disciplines even when their own, traditional field is concerned.

There can be only one solution: to dissociate state and church more fully, and to re-organize the study of religion in the German state universities. There should be departments of religion (with sub- departments of Christian studies and biblical studies) which employ professors exclusively on the basis of academic merit and integrity rather than on the basis of ecclesiastical affiliation and orthodoxy. Even the churches, or so I hope, would have more respect for independent academic teachers than for professorial members of their own clergy. To sum up: the Lüdemann case reveals that German university departments of theology enjoy no proper academic status. Therefore they should be first abolished, and then reorganized according to different rules.

This cannot happen without a severe crisis, and my sincere hope is that such a crisis will actually take place. "Crises and even their accompanying fanaticisms are to be regarded as genuine signs of vitality." Jacob Burckhardt (1818-1897), the cultural historian who included this statement in his famous Reflections on History, adds an apt description of a crisis such as the one I have in mind: "Crises clear the ground, firstly of a host of institutions from which life has long since departed, and which, given their historical privilege, could not be swept away in any other fashion. Further, of true pseudo-organisms which ought never to have existed, but which had nevertheless, in the course of time, gained a firm hold upon the fabric of life, and were, indeed, mainly to blame for the preference of mediocrity and the hatred of excellence."

9

The Gentilemen's Agreement

Amy-Jill Levine

Vanderbilt University Divinity School and the Graduate Department of Religion

In her classic novel, Laura Z. Hobson described how genteel society maintained its restricted neighborhoods, businesses, and clubs through a "Gentlemen's Agreement."[1] The agreement was simply presupposed, and everyone knew it. No law was needed; no signs reading "Niggers, Jews, and dogs unwelcome" were posted, although occasionally the more polite term "Restricted" did appear. The agreement prevailed in the academy as well: while those "not of the right type" were refused admission, children of alumni were welcomed through an unspoken affirmative action based not only on select ethnic, racial, and religious identifications,[2] but also on class status. The Agreement was exacerbated on those campuses where sororities and fraternities determined social policy and insiders chose their colleagues via the unfortunately albeit aptly named system of "black-balling." Today the system continues, occasionally masked by token enfranchisement and frequently profiting from similarly restricted neighborhoods, businesses and clubs built by and for those made unwelcome elsewhere.

---

[1] Hobson, Laura Keane Zametkin, *Gentleman's Agreement, A Novel* (New York, Simon and Schuster, 1947).

[2] The reason so many American Jews, usually highly in favor of liberal social policies, split with their political companions on the issue of quotas is their memory of "Jew quotas" held by certain college and university admission officers: Jews were refused admittance to many institutions of higher education because they were Jewish.

Compared to this tacit system, the German academy should be applauded: they do not hide the criteria that determine who may belong to which club or who may teach in what program: Christian theists are welcome in Theology Departments; atheists as well non-Christian children of Abraham are not. Honesty is certainly preferable to smug silence.

Within the context of the United States, some undergraduate Departments of Religion as well as seminaries designed to prepare students for the ministry have, like the German system, explicit theological requirements. My concern, however, is with the Gentleman's Agreement in institutions of higher education that promote themselves as not restrained to or by any confession but rather as having an ethos of open inquiry.[3] American Collegiate Departments of Religion (which teach undergraduates) and University-based Divinity schools (with a graduate student clientele)have been known to maintain their own parochial system, which might be called the *Gentleman's* Agreement. Originally, like the rest of the faculty at their schools, faculty comprising these programs were male, white, and Christian. University-based Divinity Schools sometimes drew upon Jewish professors from Arts and Science Departments of Religion or from Graduate Programs to supplement their own courses, but such faculty would not hold a joint appointment (conversely, Christian Professors of New Testament in Arts and Science Departments may well hold a joint appointment with a Divinity School).[4]

These were days when white Christian men taught everything; "women's studies" and "Jewish Studies" didn't exist; African-American studies was limited to a few references in history courses to Martin Luther King, Jr.; Asia was ignored. Finally, during the 1960s and 1970s, women, men and women of Asian and African descent, and others from groups with co-opted histories gained both programs dedicated to their identities as well as teaching positions in such programs. The benefits of such programs extended beyond the broadening of the academic enterprise to personal affirmation: students from such groups now had role models who "look like them." Having attended a women's college, I can personally testify to the importance of seeing someone who "looked like me" at the lectern. When these multicultural doors opened, a number of Departments of Religion then

---

[3] The ethos of open inquiry is not mutually exclusive to a program or school with a specific religious identification; one can work in the training of students for a particular ministry and at the same time challenge certain views of that particular church; an adherent to one tradition can train students who will be ordained in another. For example, Fr. Roland Murphy, O. Carm., taught for years at the United Methodist Duke Divinity School.

[4] Lou Silberman took Samuel Sandmel's position at Vanderbilt in 1952; his appointment was in the Graduate School; "Silberman became officially part of the Divinity School faculty in 1964, although he had had an office in the school and had been at least informally acknowledged as a member of the faculty from the time of his appointment." See Peter J. Haas, "Jewish Studies," in Dale A. Johnson (ed.), *Vanderbilt Divinity School: Education, Contest, and Change* (Nashville, TN: Vanderbilt University Press, 2001), p. 305.

explicitly promulgated a "you are what you teach" model: Muslims teach Islam; Buddhists teach Buddhism; Jews teach Judaism, etc. This intentionality in hiring was premised on a call for justice: just as certain groups were privileged in the past, so a deliberate advancement of other groups became demanded in the present. This model of faculty hiring still prevails in many institutions of higher education.

The benefits of a multicultural curriculum and of a faculty that can speak from various social locations are enormous. However, a program can gain this type of diversity without the stereotyping that underlies the "you are what you teach" model. Indeed, this model, especially today, has numerous problems. First are the dangers of what is frequently called "identity politics": hiring so identified with one's racial, religious, ethnic, gendered, or sexual identity signals to students that *only* insiders, indeed only special insiders who meet particular demographic categories, can speak about a particular topic. Thus, the ideal of open inquiry, the ideal of a *university*, is compromised. Second is the epistemological question: to what extent does personal identity ordain special authority for addressing issues outside direct experience? Is the twenty-first century African-American better qualified to teach the African-American history than a Chinese-American colleague? Must those teaching Caribbean literature be of Caribbean descent?

These questions become increasingly acute when posed to ideological or confessional rather than racial categories: must those who teach Marxism be Marxist? Those who teach theology be theists? Is the twenty-first century Christian in a better position to teach Christianity, let alone Christian origins, than a Jew? Conversely (if facetiously), should one argue that, since Jesus, James, Peter, and Paul were all Jews, the teaching of Christian origins should be done by Jews?

Despite problems both political and academic, one could make a cogent argument that the answer to al of these questions must be "Yes". Some might argue that the study of Christianity should retain the same sort of privilege claimed by other groups both in prior decades and today: women should teach women's studies, gay people teach "Queer theory," Asians teach Asian history, Christians should teach Christianity, and only Christian theists should teach in a program that trains representatives of the Church. These are not, however, arguments I can support.

On the confessional front, there is no need for Christian affirmative action. The Church has not typically had its traditions co-opted, or prepackaged into another's categories, so there is no need for a rectification of past prejudice.[5] Further, in Western institutions is there no shortage of Christian role models. Nor, if we take academics seriously, is there any reason why an outsider cannot teach a particular text or tradition with both empathy and accuracy. One need not believe

---

[5] There are exceptions: the presentation of Roman Catholicism by Protestant scholars (especially in Seminaries and Divinity Schools) and, (often less problematic), the teaching of the various Protestant traditions by Roman Catholics. Eastern Orthodoxy is absent from most Western curricula.

in the resurrection of Jesus in order to present accurately the beliefs of those who do, any more than one need believe in the literal creation of the world in seven days in order to present historically, cross-culturally, aesthetically, and theologically, Genesis 1 or even to give an account of the Creationist position. Faculty should fairly and generously present positions with which they disagree. In the study of Religion and of Theology, the student needs to know not only what a particular group thought or did, but also what the various options were; heresy is only determined in retrospect. If faculty challenge conventional wisdom, good; academics is the site for intellectual inquiry, not for training either sponges or clones.

Nevertheless, the prevailing desideratum for the teaching of Christianity, and especially for the study of the New Testament, remains even in the United States one of affirmative action for the privileged. In an academic version of the U.S. military's policy concerning homosexuality – known as "don't ask, don't tell – those Departments of Religion and Divinity Schools that do not require members to sign a confession of faith typically presume the person teaching New Testament or Christian origins to be Christian. While the Asian professor is clearly identifiable by race, the woman by gender, the Jew often by last name or explicit self-disclosure (e.g., through dress, diet, Sabbath observance), the default identification of those teaching Christianity in general, New Testament in particular, is Christian. Complicating this presumed identification is the form of Christianity espoused by the New Testament or theology instructor: those schools which profess the ideal of open inquiry also often do not want faculty who are *too* Christian: church membership is fine, but active proselytizers for a particular brand of (usually Conservative) Christianity are less welcome.

As with the situation in Göttingen, problems in the mainstream U.S. educational system's teaching of Christianity emerge when potential faculty members make explicit their dissociation from Christian identity, for example, by rejecting a special soteriological role for Jesus, or by formally noting their affiliation with an alternative tradition. In instances where the candidate's affiliation may be unclear, an unclarity most easily created by a non-Christian-sounding name (e.g., Mohammed, Levine), the cautious phone call is often made. In the early 1980s, a potential employer with a position open in biblical studies queried a member of my dissertation committee: "Just how Jewish is she?" The member responded, "I suppose she's more Jewish than some and less than others." Given American civility, neither party delineated what "Jewish" meant: level of *halachic* observance; stereotypical cultural identification (would she fit in a predominantly upper-middle class Protestant town); a viable role model for Jewish students? The question would not, I suspect, have been posed about someone Christian.

In the U.S. system, such inquiries about religious identification are illegal; we are no more to discriminate on the basis of religion than we are in any other form of non-sectarian hiring or housing. But the call from that first employer is by no means unique. "How Jewish is she?" is not an unanticipated question, especially when the subject matter is Christianity. The same point works in reverse for hiring in Jewish studies, and especially if the position is an endowed Chair: "Is he Jewish? How Jewish is he?"

This concern for appropriate identification for faculty membership is not limited to the department or school. The hiring of a non-Christian for a position in Christian studies (New Testament; Christian theology) also creates concern among the school's supporters or neighbors, both Christian and not. Hire a Jew to teach New Testament, and some members of the local Jewish community become agitated: Is the candidate a "Jew for Jesus"? Will she proselytize? Likewise, some Christians will fear that such a professor seeks to undermine their tradition. Not one of these issues would be posed about or to a candidate who at least, by name, appears to be Christian.

Even if a non-traditional hire is made, such as the appointing of a Jew to teach Christian origins or an atheist to teach theology, the university ideal of open inquiry need not be fulfilled. At Vanderbilt Divinity School, every year a few ministerial candidates refuse to take courses on Christian texts taught by those who are explicitly members of a religious community other than the Christian church. Yet they never ask the (nominally) Christian faculty about their religious beliefs or practices. Ironically, the faculty member explicitly associated with a religious tradition may be closer to these students in orientation and concerns, but — so the students think — better a tacit atheist than an overt Jew. Such students would be more at home in those denominational seminaries where the faculty sign statements of orthodoxy (that Jesus condemned oaths as inappropriate and that he insisted "it is not those who say 'Lord Lord' but those who do the will of the Father" who are to be commended is needs to be ignored in such cases). Positively, their concern translates into intensive respect for creedal materials coupled with the notion that insiders can present a system better than outsiders can.[6] Negatively, it suggests a preference for a self-congratulatory and potentially ossified system where insularity replaces intellectual inquiry.

Divinity Schools and Department of Religion who hire faculty outside the confessional basis of the majority have certain scholastic advantages. Such faculty may be more likely to insist on clear articulation of theological proclamations rather than accept what within Christian discourse is presumed; they may be more sensitive to matters of triumphalism, anti-Judaism, and cultural hegemony; they may be better able to inculcate in students an appreciation for (or at least a breaking of negative stereotypes concerning) alternative religious traditions and perspectives; they may make the outsider feel more welcome in the classroom, and therefore

---

[6] There are Jewish and Muslim schools with the same ethos; insularity and self-congratulation are not traits unique to Christianity.

open the study beyond those who are "believers and would-be believers."[7] These results prevail at Vanderbilt. While there are, as noted, a few students who will not work with non-Christian faculty, *the vast majority not only appreciate the alternative voices, their grappling with diverse views makes them better representatives of their own traditions.*

Were an atheist to teach a course in Christian theology, those who seek to preserve Christianity have nothing to worry about (any more than they should worry that Christianity will vanish if carols are taken out of U.S. elementary school winter concerts). Orthodoxy will always have its representatives: the demographics of who are receiving Ph.D.s and who are interested in and competent at teaching in Divinity Schools and Religion Departments guarantees this. If a non-Christian presents the material under study sympathetically (one does not have to believe in the resurrection of Jesus to address how the claim is important to Paul or Matthew), there is no problem. Even were an atheist to deliver a lecture arguing that Jesus' body was eaten by dogs,[8] the church will not topple. In an atmosphere of open inquiry and intellectual engagement, students as well as faculty are free to express their opinions, and some students may well take exception to the lecture. Moreover, If such a lecture causes a student to question theological presuppositions, good; considered faith is stronger faith. If a de-emphasis on the resurrection allows a student more fully to esteem the material that appears between Jesus' birth and his death (i.e., the material omitted from the creeds), good again; the whole world would do well to pay attention to Jesus' teachings of nonviolence, advocacy of economic redistribution, and love of Torah. A bit more honesty and a bit less hypocrisy are traits Jesus would have appreciated.

---

[7] A statement on the syllabus for "Themes in the New Testament" taught under the auspices of the Dept. of Religious Studies (not the Divinity School) at Vanderbilt University.

[8] "But you did not return because your resurrection was only a pious wish. This is certain, because your body rotted in the tomb — that is, if it was put in a tomb at all and not devoured by vultures and jackals." Gerd Lüdemann, *The Great Deception and What Jesus Really Said and Did* (London: SCM, 1998; translation of *Der grosse Betrug. Und was Jesus wirklich sagte und tat* [Dietrich zu Klampen Verlag GbR, 1998]), p. 3.

10

Jacob Neusner

Bard College

Walking the streets of Göttingen with Gerd Lüdemann when I was Von Humboldt Visiting Research Professor in the Theology Faculty in the summer semester of 1995, I could always sense his pride in the tradition of academic theology that he himself carried forward. He would take pleasure in pointing out the house where one or another of the great names of that world-class theological tradition had resided. Each one triggered a conversation on what endured of their protean contributions. Not only so, but the present faculty includes important and influential figures, who accorded me a cordial welcome. All the more reason to regret what has come to pass, the scandal that has called into question the academic integrity of Göttingen scholarship in religion and theology.

To be sure, even then, I did not find the students impressive. When one of them interrupted me in a seminar early in the semester to announce with outrage, "You talk too much," I concurred, took my coat, walked out, canceled the seminar for the rest of the semester, and never entered a Göttingen class room again. But that did not diminish my esteem for the academic ambience, past and present. I dismissed the students from my mind as not-house-broken (*salon-fahig*). I saw considerably more abusive conduct when I lectured at Yale. Thuggery in the class room marks the malady of the age, not the peculiar trait of German theology students, to act like boors.

Despite the pretensions of Hengel's rather second-rate Tübingen, Göttingen possessed Germany's premier tradition in theology and New Testament studies. In the university of Wellhausen, Schürer, Bauer, Jeremias, Käsemann and Conzelmann, censorship of scholarship must be unthinkable. Imagine my surprise, therefore, to learn that, in reprisal for the content of his scholarship and teaching ("renouncing Christianity"), taking leave of its own profound tradition of free inquiry, the Theology faculty sought to separate Lüdemann from his position as credentialed teacher of Theology students and researcher within that faculty. That the issue is scholarship, not theological conviction, is made explicit by the faculty statement: "we dispute that these statements are the necessary conclusions to be drawn from scientific insights." That is a perfectly honorable position: all of us argue all the time. Contention animates our lives. But then one must allow for every conclusion and its opposite. If we know in advance what conclusions we are required to reach, our scholarship loses all integrity. We take as our task the defense of dogma, not the inquiry into truth. I will not argue with someone if my mind is not open to his proposition; it is not honest.

But that assumes at issue is academic learning, not the certification of correct opinions. And it further takes for granted that academic theology is academic, not an exercise in catechism. Göttingen's faculty declares itself not academic in its character, and vocational in its calling: studying a subject only to prepare people correctly to teach required dogmas about that subject. That premise as to its own character explains why Lüdemann has been removed from the work of educating pastors and teachers of Protestant Christianity. The New Testament and earliest Christianity now are represented only by those who affirm their narratives, not those who propose critically to analyze them: a work of recapitulation, not critical, independent re-presentation. And the transaction transcends merely symbolic sanctions. Lüdemann furthermore finds himself penalized: no students, no degree program, no research support. Not only so, but the Theology faculties elsewhere in Germany have chosen to join in the boycott and administrative excommunication. His books are not reviewed, his students, now refugees, are not accepted in other degree programs, so are penalized for their first teacher's sins.

Lüdemann correctly phrases the matter in academic terms: "an intrinsic contradiction for academic theology on the one hand to claim for itself the epithet 'scientific,' and on the other hand to subserve the goals and principles of the church." "My colleagues do not recognize the possible tension...between scientific judgments and judgments of faith." Now an oath is required, which excludes from the Theology faculty all but Lutheran believers. The study of Judaism is closed off to faithful Jews, of Islam to practicing Muslims. Göttingen's appointment for the study of Judaism is not yet among its more distinguished professors and voted with the majority that dismissed Lüdemann on doctrinal grounds.

No one can have framed the issue more fundamentally than does Lüdemann himself when he points out three facts. First, the Theology faculty itself departs significantly from the faith. Second, the academic study of religion "hardly exists in German universities." Third, "as long as theology remains in the university, it has to research and inform, not reveal and preach."

The one point on which he is to be corrected is his insistence on speaking of Germany as though corresponding conditions and restrictions upon the academy in the name of religion and its orthodoxies flourished only there. But in the world of Judaism and of Islam, counterpart conduct is commonplace. Indeed, administrative excommunication of persons of improper opinion, death by silence (Tot-schweigen), and campaigns of character-assassination and demonization corrupt academic discourse under Jewish auspices; I leave it to Catholics to speak for themselves; and as to the universities of Islam, to speak of academic freedom in teaching and learning is to ask what is unthinkable. He points to the destructive impact of censorship upon the academic study of religion in Germany. In the secular Jewish university, Brandeis, and in the Orthodox Jewish university, Yeshiva University, the academic study of religion does not even exist. And the manifest weakness of the discipline in the state of Israel, with only a handful of practitioners of any standing to begin with, hardly suggests a greater appreciation for *Lernfreiheit* and *Lehrfreiheit* in the academy under Jewish auspices than in the German universities. The intellectual price of teaching at Bar Ilan University is not only orthopraxy (wearing a head covering at all times), but avoidance of dangerous subjects, such as biblical criticism, insistence on a heavy burden of positivism and above all a persistent process of repeating in one's own words what the holy books say, all in the name of history.

So Lüdemann's honesty raises the question: is theology possible in the academy? And if so, under what protocols?

Since I hold a research professorship in theology, not only in religion, I clearly maintain that full freedom of inquiry enjoys compatibility with the study of the belief-systems and truths of practiced religions. Theology, meaning, the rigorous study of the system and logic of a religion and the criticism thereof, is possible in three academic settings: the description of the history of theology and the theological systems of a given religious tradition; the analysis of the structure(s) of theology and theological systems as exercises in an unfolding logic; and the interpretation of theology in the this-worldly context of society, politics, and culture, ancient and contemporary. These represent philosophical studies of the ideas that people hold who form communities of faithful, and they define a vital exercise in cultural study.

What of constructive theology, what of systematic theology — and the necessary advocacy of theological truth as truth, not merely the analysis of theological truth as a cultural artifact? It is difficult to deny a place to advocacy in theology, when we protect the work of philosophers to teach (their) philosophy, not only about philosophy. I cannot recall anyone's objecting to political scientists' expressing their views on public policy. It is part of their vocation of intellect. Historians form judgments of the past and make their weightiest contribution to learning when they dare to express opinions.

What has gone wrong in Göttingen is an excess of low-brow vocationalism: an insistence that all teaching in the Theology faculty aims at training pastors and Church school teachers, and that for a particular Church. The premise is, the only audience for learning in religion and theology is the future advocates of religion and theology, not persons of culture and broad sympathy, not people for whom religion and theology represent components of culture and ornaments of civilization.

The academic study of Religion in British, Canadian, American, Australian and New Zealand universities takes its position within the humanities and does not pretend to qualify its students to serve a particular Church or religion for that matter. No one assumes that the students must emerge able to transmit a particular doctrine, only that they understand, in a this-worldly framework, a vital component of the social order of all known civilizations and cultures. In the pre-professional setting of theology at Göttingen, it is entirely plausible to tell a professor he is talking too much — and saying the wrong things. In that context it is completely reasonable to insist that all professors on the Theology faculty must be Protestants.

We must never underestimate the enduring consequences of the National Socialist period in the history and tradition of the German universities — even to the third and fourth generations later. Nor can we overestimate the power of the academy to realize its intellectual promise and to accomplish its tasks of criticism and research, when religion is at stake. Göttingen proves the first of these propositions, the universities under Jewish auspices, the second. But the academic study of religion addresses the single most powerful force in civilization, present and past. It is too critical a subject to leave the study of religions to the religions themselves — and not to undertake to study not only religions, but religion, which only the academy can accomplish. That is what is at stake in the career-crisis of Professor Lüdemann.

11

Vocational Schools, Professor Lüdemann, and the University: Lessons from the American Law School Experience and Mark Twain

Stephen B. Presser

Do vocational schools belong in the University? This is really the question posed by the events surrounding the removal of Gerd Lüdemann from his chair in New Testament Theology. The issues, as put by Professor Lüdemann go to the nature of the University and to the nature of academic freedom. Can a faculty which limits its members to those who agree to subscribe to a particular set of religious dogmas really be manifesting the kind of scientific inquiry and commitment to objective truth that ought to be found in a University setting? Should academic freedom – the purported ideology of the University – dictate that those whose scholarship compels them to the conclusion that Christianity gets it wrong nevertheless have standing to remain as members of a Christian theological faculty? A similar *cause celebre* to that of Professor Lüdemann occurred in the American Legal Academy in the mid-eighties, and, if there are lessons from that brouhaha, they are probably that (1) Professor Lüdemann belongs in the university, but not on the theological faculty, and (2) that the theological faculty, even if it is a "vocational school," still belongs in the University.

In 1984, the then Dean of Duke University's School of Law, Paul Carrington, published, in the Journal of Legal Education (a relatively non-scholarly journal devoted to articles of pedagogical interest to law professors), a provocative piece called "Of Law and the River." Carrington attacked a group of people whom he labeled "Legal Nihilists," whom he accused of believing that the Rule of Law (which he defined, more or less, as the notion that law could actually restrain "the lash of power") was a myth. These Legal Nihilists, explained Carrington, took the position that law was simply a tool of the powerful, to be manipulated for their own purposes. This probably meant, Carrington seemed to suggest, that these "Legal Nihilists" believed that it was permissible, or at least understandable, for lawyers to use the malevolent arts of chicanery, fraud, and corruption in the service of their clients, particularly where the clients were the downtrodden and powerless. People who believed that the rule of law was a myth and the tool of the powerful, Carrington argued, might have a place in the university – presumably in Sociology or Political Science Departments — but they didn't belong in Law Schools. To teach in a Law School, Carrington explained, if one was to pass on to lawyers in training the proper professional ethos, one had to have, as he put it, a "romantic faith" that the rule of law was real; that law actually did serve justice and actually did restrain the powerful. The most important things about training lawyers, Carrington argued, were to inculcate in them belief in the rule of law, to foster their legal "judgment and courage," and to discourage them from cynicism. Such cynicism, he believed, would lead to dishonest, fraudulent, and corrupt recourse to manipulation of arcane legal doctrines and procedures to serve their personal ends or the selfish interests of their clients.

The required kind of teaching could not be done by Legal Nihilists, Carrington explained, because their own cynicism would disable them from passing on the proper professional "romantic faith." The content of that "romantic faith," apart from a belief in the rule of law, was a bit obscure, although Carrington also likened it to the requirements of training for river pilots which Mark Twain described in his *Life on the Mississippi*, hence the title of Carrington's piece. Twain, the young "cub," was relentlessly hectored and bullied by his pilot teacher, one Horace Bixby, into learning the arcane and difficult skills of a Mississippi Riverboat Captain, not by honeyed praise for doing well, but by the application of unceasing criticism. This turned Twain into a great pilot because he had unbounded respect and admiration for Bixby, who did manifest extraordinary technical skill, and who also manifested spectacular pride (amounting nearly to arrogance) in his professional skill and responsibilities. Carrington's notion seemed to be that just as there was a "romance" about the trade of pilot – Twain likened them to kings, as when they were on the river their authority was unchallenged, and they were responsible for the life or death of every passenger put in their charge – there ought to be a similar romance about the trade of lawyer. As do Mississippi River pilots, lawyers, as manipulators of the institutions of the law, possess great power and responsibility, and often have the lives of their clients in their hands. They need, as do pilots, Carrington maintained, to take pride in their profession, and to develop the judgment and courage properly to carry out their responsibilities. There was some mystery in Carrington's presentation, but the business about Twain's hectoring teacher was a very effective defense of the Socratic method in the law schools, the sometimes brutal teaching technique then in vogue there, and an attack on those (the Legal Nihilists? The student radicals of the Vietnam era and beyond?) who were demanding what they called "the no-hassle pass," allowing them to opt out of being on the receiving end of the Socratic method. The Socratic method, the testing of law students by rhetorical fire, Carrington suggested, taught them how to think on their feet, and forced them to learn the judgment and courage necessary to be good lawyers.

Though Carrington never specified who he meant by the "Legal Nihilists," it quickly became clear that he had in mind some practitioners of something called "the Conference on Critical Legal Studies," a newly-emerged group of law professors, especially at Harvard, Yale, and Stanford, who were trying, as their name implied, to apply the insights of the Frankfurt School's "Critical theory," to the study of American law. The Conference on Critical Legal Studies, or "CLS," or the "Crits," as they soon became known, struck back in a variety of ways, chiefly along two fronts. One was to deny that they were in fact "Legal Nihilists," as Carrington defined the term, and the other was to decry the McCarthyite implications of the kind of "loyalty oath" that Carrington seemed to be demanding. In short, the Crits refused to emigrate to sociology departments, and worried about whether their younger colleagues were likely to get tenure, especially in the non-elite law schools. Eventually CLS collapsed of its own weight when its socialist and redistributionist credo lost cachet following the fall of the Berlin Wall. In the meantime, though, Carrington replied to his critics by claiming that at least some of those associated with CLS did indeed appear to believe that the rule of law was a fraud, and by asking – *mirabile dictu* – whether it wasn't obvious that Legal Nihilists should be barred from teaching in law schools just as it was obvious that an atheist should be barred from teaching in a divinity school.

This question – should an atheist be allowed to teach in a divinity school? – is one I annually ask my legal history students (to whom I assign Carrington's essay and that of one of his critics where this point is discussed). Most of my students are convinced that atheists should not be barred from the faculty of divinity schools, just as they believe that Crits should not be barred from law schools. They would have a great deal of sympathy for Professor Lüdemann. The majority of these American law students are good late twentieth century liberals, and believe in the maxim "different strokes for different folks." They hold, with John Stuart Mill, that the truth ought to battle constantly with falsehood, lest it get flabby. It's good for divinity school students to listen to the arguments of atheists, my students explain; it will strengthen their faith, or perhaps convince them they don't belong in divinity school after all. It's good for law students to listen to those critical of the law, even good for law students to be exposed to radicals who believe the whole legal system is a sham; it's good to listen to everyone's arguments, and everyone is entitled to his or her own beliefs. That's the theory of our First Amendment and our commitment to freedom of speech, after all – let a thousand arguments bloom. And then I ask them, "All right, maybe you want to see atheists in divinity schools, and Crits in law schools. Would you permit people *who don't believe in the river* to teach pilots?" That tends to give them some pause.

And that, perhaps, was Carrington's real point. To create a real professional commitment in impressionable young student minds, perhaps the teacher has to have some faith, whether it's in the Rule of Law, or Christianity, or the wet reality of the Mississippi. This is probably not an assertion easily subject to objective proof, and perhaps only those who share a commitment to a professional ethos which springs from something more than rationality will understand it. The word "vocation," as originally used, meant "calling," and is derivative of the Latin verb, *Vocare*, "to call." "Vocation," still shows up in modern dictionaries as having the meaning of "a function or station in life to which one is called by God." Both the ministry and the study of law were, as recently as a generation ago, frequently referred to as "callings," and the idea was that one was drawn to them, probably by God, but certainly by something more than mere rationality or logic. There is no denying that many great theologians, past and present, believed that logic and science are perfectly compatible with religious belief, but surely there are some elements of religion, or religious calling, that must be accepted on faith, and the merely human tools of science and rationality are inadequate to prove or even to refute them. Or at least such a belief might be necessary in those with the responsibility to turn out future leaders in religion or the law. What Twain was trying to say about great river pilots, what Carrington was trying to say about law professors, and what Professor Lüdemann denies with respect to theology teachers, is that when one trains professionals, one must teach by example, and teaching and believing in articles of faith is a part of preparing one to execute a calling.

Whatever the complex legal and political relationships among the Ministry of Science and Culture in Lower Saxony, the churches of the Confederation of Protestant Churches in Lower Saxony, the University of Göttingen and its theological faculty — as a matter of professional theory, if not professional morality, if not professional need, it seems appropriate for Professor Lüdemann to practice his scholarship in a way that doesn't involve a responsibility for preparing people to minister to those of a faith to which he no longer subscribes. *He doesn't, in short, believe in the river, and he shouldn't be training pilots.*

But to give Professor Lüdemann credit for the consistency of his own beliefs, and his commitment to the enterprise of scholarship and the search for truth, he appears to conceive of a faculty of theology in quite different terms. He believes that in a University all should be free to pursue where their scholarly inquiries take them, and none should be expelled from one University branch simply because one's beliefs change. To require oaths of belief of Professor Lüdemann, so the argument runs, is to infringe on his academic freedom, and to reveal a commitment to something other than objective scientific truth. But that commitment to something other than scientific truth is precisely the nature of a vocation, or, dare we say it, a vocational school like Law or Theology. If the Universities are to be training grounds for the professions, and not just training grounds for professors of what we Americans refer to as the "Liberal Arts" (e.g. philosophy, literature, the sciences, politics, history, etc.), there is a limit to the individual academic freedom of those that teach in the professional schools.

With the responsibility of a teacher of professionals comes a commitment to the profession and its received professional credos. One can certainly dismiss them as "dogmas," or deride them as "myths," but they have a reality, a force, and a nobility understood by those who are committed to the profession or the calling and what they stand for. There is, of course, value, even in the professions, for independence of thought and free inquiry, but there are limits. Indeed, even in the Liberal Arts (or "Arts and Sciences") departments, some individual conclusions probably go too far – should a Black Studies department be required to retain a White supremacist, or a Jewish Studies department a holocaust denier? These last examples are probably not precisely on point, but they illustrate a fundamental truth about universities – that, as their name implies, they are about more than individuals. They are about passing on knowledge, and about passing on cultural values. In Western culture, among those values are the importance of scientific inquiry and academic freedom of individuals, but also among those values are the professional creeds of service to others (prominent in medicine and law, as well as the ministry), and fidelity to professional credos ("do no harm," serve justice, serve God). These professional creeds are about much more than individualism, and I wonder if this is fully understood by Professor Lüdemann. Professor Lüdemann has a carefully-constructed and fully thought-out vision of what a theology department ought to be, but it is an idiosyncratic notion given the understanding of his colleagues, of the Church, and of the ministry.

We in America tend to take individualism pretty far, so far, in fact, that our Supreme Court, in a case purportedly involving a "right to privacy," uttered what is probably the single stupidest pronouncement ever made by three judges. In its three-person plurality opinion in Planned Parenthood v. Casey (1992), in the course of a dubious holding that the Constitution contained a right for women to have abortions, the Supreme Court opined, in what has come to be known as the "mystery passage," that "At the heart of liberty is the right to define one's own concept of existence, of meaning, of the universe, and of the mystery of human life." But meaning in life doesn't come through one's totally individualized insight, meaning comes from the culture, and cannot be found without the aid of and through relationships with others. Universities exist to search for knowledge, and to search for knowledge in many different ways, and certainly promoting free individual inquiry is a worthy endeavor at the university. But there are others.

The great vocational schools, the training grounds for lawyers, doctors, and ministers, also perform a function well-suited to the university in passing on the great values of service to others of the culture. In Western Culture, after all, it is the task of the learned professions, surely, to transmit the culture and its highest altruistic values. Just as individuals have some academic freedom, those vocational schools have a sort of collective institutional right to freedom to decide how to transmit those values, and to decide what those values ought to be, and, it would seem, there are some occasions when the vocational schools must make the painful choice that an absence of one or more of these values on the part of one who would seek to train professional students disqualifies that one from teaching. The faculty of theology belongs at Göttingen, and Professor Lüdemann's right to academic freedom ought to be viewed as guaranteeing him no more than a place in his university, but not on the faculty of theology.

12

Robert M. Price

Center for Inquiry Institute

In a time of comfortably orthodox retrenchment among New Testament scholars, Gerd Lüdemann has been a bracing voice urging scholars not to forget, as they seem eager to do, the radical insights of David Friedrich Strauss. Lüdemann stands courageously for Strauss's brand of intellectual honesty. And like Strauss who was ejected from the teaching profession, Lüdemann is now paying the price. Like the ancient Sanhedrin closing ranks against Jesus (why do they never even notice the parallel?), the Protestant authorities at Göttingen University have decreed that Professor Lüdemann shall lose research funding and that divinity students shall no longer study with him. Thankfully, he has not yet been consigned to the streets.

Lüdemann's "crime" was to leap from the confining nest of Mother Church and to take wing with the pinions of critical reason and spiritual honesty. Long since having repudiated biblical literalism, he recently found theological liberalism equally galling. He could no longer brook the pretense that Jesus rose from the dead in some Pickwickian sense compatible with his corpse rotting, that the Christian should live in "eschatological hope" (the charade of Lent), even though the promise of the Parousia is over nineteen centuries forfeit. As Socrates urged his disciples to think not of Socrates but only of the truth, Lüdemann at last decided that the truth itself was the only banner he could fly in good conscience. And this the Göttingen Sanhedrin deems thought-crime, a contagion from which tender seminarians must be shielded.

Some might regret Lüdemann's treatment and yet grant that an institution has a right not to employ those unsympathetic to its official policy. Jello could no longer be expected to pay for Bill Cosby's endorsement if he made it known he preferred Royal Gelatin instead. In this manner some likewise defended the Pope's decision, some years ago, to forbid Hans Küng to teach any longer at Tübingen as a "Professor of Catholic Theology." But this defense is fatally revealing, is it not? For it is a bald-faced admission of the very crime with which Lüdemann has implicitly charged the Church: preferring a particular party-line, a given set of opinions, to the truth per se. Is the truth material, a set of dogmas we already possess? Or is it formal, a North Star by which to navigate our search? If the truth is not open-ended, it is hypocritical to pretend to search for it. And that is the pretense (if that is all it is) of great universities such as Göttingen and Tübingen have been. But of late they seem enamored of becoming indoctrination mills, glorified Bible colleges. The difference is exactly that between academic freedom and intellectual honesty on the one hand and mere catechism on the other. To condemn Lüdemann because he won't "get with the program" as a loyally gray apparatchik shows where his university stands.

We as Humanists, including Gerd Lüdemann, do not share the Christian faith, however much we may respect it. But we may be said to embrace a faith of our own: the confidence, perhaps naive, that the truth will come out. It must evidence its superiority in the contest of ideas. This is why we do not try to "protect" ourselves/ our students from any knowledge from any source. We trust the free and inquiring mind to make its own responsible choice. Apparently religious institutions like Göttingen University eschew that faith. But they betray their own as well, since they must deem the Christian faith of seminarians too brittle to withstand the impact of critical scholarship like Lüdemann's. Ironically, by their action, the good Christian elders of Göttingen have only vindicated Gerd Lüdemann's decision to leave his Christian allegiance behind. In the process they have confirmed our long-held suspicion as well: ultimately a religious creed and intellectual honesty must act each upon the other as fire and water.

13

A Catholic Perspective on Protestant Göttingen

William Shea

St. Louis University

If Professor Lüdemann were to go elsewhere, we could say "Lüdemann's gain, Göttingen's loss." But if he cannot and things at Goettingen continue on their present course everyone loses. Lüdemann's personal and professional loss is serious enough to raise the hair on any professor's neck. The loss to the university is great in terms of its students and its integrity. I know nothing of its theology faculty there, but I can imagine with very little stretch my own faculty of theological studies behaving in the same way in a similar situation.

I argued over twenty years ago in "The Subjectivity of the Theologian" that "without orthodox Christian belief theology may still be good theology." This puts me in Lüdemann's corner if the issue is what makes a theologian an academic theologian. In my view a confession of ecclesiastical faith is not basic requisite. And Lüdemann has fulfilled what I see as the basic conditions of academic theology: (1) an intense scholarly interest in his/her religious tradition and (2) in the issues of truth in that tradition as well as of its meaning.

A theologian who then publicly renounces his share the church's belief has, in a peculiar way, offered irrefutable proof of intense interest when the renunciation is added to a continuing stream of research important in the field. This is Lüdemann's case as I understand it. Surely it would help the problem of communication if he/she did not despise the faith and its practitioners, and in fact sympathized with and even admired them, but that is beside the basic point. A lack of belief in the truth claims of that tradition should not be made to cancel one's academic standing as a theologian, though it cancels theological standing in the church. One would have hoped that Lüdemann's colleagues were capable of this distinction. Alas, for them as well as for him, they were not. Perhaps Lüdemann and I and they are caught, and ever shall be, between the university and the church in this respect.

Churches are not founded on academic insights or conclusions about Moses' conversation with G__ on Sinai, Jesus' resurrection, Mohammed's experiences in the cave, or Joseph Smith's golden plates. The religious communities don't take to the sort of basic criticism that is Lüdemann's academic trade. The church (or synagogue or mosque) does not support scholars or teachers who say goodbye to the facticity of the event and to the truth of the text, and it does not like to see tax money supporting these scholars either. Again, why should we be surprised by or chagrined at the refusal of the church to allow an unbeliever to form the mind of ministerial students, no matter how well credentialed or even how well disposed the professor may be? It is not hard to imagine the upset of donors of a dedicated business school at an American university should a chair holder say a principled goodbye to capitalism.

Universities are not impregnable redoubts of pure scholarly conversation; they have to fight for their identity in their sometimes hostile environment, within in and without the gates. Think of the outrages that linguistic philosophers and postmodernists have worked in philosophy and literature departments over the past half century, forcing professors into unwelcome retirement and closing the doors to the ideologically unbaptized newcomers. One might say that the church has no right to hold the faculty member hostage to its beliefs, but then faculties of all subjects hold students and colleagues hostage to their own ideologically inspired academic beliefs. The latter is so directly and obviously a contradiction to the liberal academic credo that one ought to be surprised and chagrined at the historical record in such matters. The lesson is that the fight goes on, and whether Lüdemann wins or loses, it will continue to go on. In this fight the church is but one concerned participant among many others. The university, after all, is the bastard child of the church and the Enlightenment, neither of which has proved hospitable to skepticism of its premises.

Theology faculties, at least those in Catholic universities and colleges, are affianced to the church. They can be likened to professional faculties even when ensconced among the humanities and social sciences which are at least professedly engaged in self-criticism. The surprise from this perspective, is not that Lüdemann has had trouble but that the other eminent Göttingeners did not. Feuerbach, if I remember correctly, could not get a chair. That a university would underwrite a theology chair for a Wilhelm Bousset is beyond church comprehension. How did the church let that slip by? Perhaps the fuss the German Protestants now make over Lüdemann is a sign that they have learned something from the Catholic church and gotten over a romance with pure academic objectivity.

The recent Catholic documents, whether from Rome or the American bishops, have been quite plain that in church affiliated Catholic universities academic freedom is to be respected "so far as the common good allows." Lüdemann understands what a church is and how it works. His complaint is evidence that he is not a Protestant or a prophet, speaking up for the truth at whatever cost. He is a professor who will not dodge and weave. He is now paying the price. You do not say goodbye to Christianity and expect applause from Christians. Compassion perhaps, applause never, and no living if it can be helped.

Surely he knows this. The church is not his issue. He does not seem to care about the church except insofar as it affects his academic locus. His problem is with the university and its failure to stand where it should, resistant to the pull of the church. So we need to talk about theology and theologians in university. As I said above, I would argue that Lüdemann is a theologian though he is not a believer. But what does a theologian do? Although there are exceptions to what appears to be the rule, the Catholic rule for theologians is that they are to be catechists so far as the university will allow them to be. For Rome and many of the American Bishops, university theologians are academically qualified, learned catechists. The Catholic Church, unlike the German Protestant churches, is facing a novelty these days: for the first time lay persons make up a large proportion of Catholic university theologians. This, I believe, is the reason why the Vatican has demanded that the bishops sponsor an unprecedented juridical bond with university theologians. As lay persons they are not subject, as clerics are, to direct ecclesiastical discipline, and Rome is determined to take the first step in so subjecting them.

In the Catholic context doubt, never mind unbelief, is a Spiritual Problem to be resolved in private *cor-ad-cor* with one's bishop or confessor (so Cardinal Ratzinger in "The Ecclesial Vocation of the Theologian"). Public profession of unbelief is incomprehensible, and challenges to belief by a university theologian are an affront to the mission of the Catholic university itself. Like in the current Protestant faculty at Göttingen, the academic theologians in an American Catholic university will not abide an unbeliever in their midst. In my own university we recently rejected a highly qualified and reputed applicant for a position in New Testament and Early Christianity because he failed an uncodified belief-and-practice test. So far as theology is concerned Saint Louis University is not an Equal Opportunity Employer! I am sure that I would not be long in the theological studies department of Saint Louis University if I said publicly "goodbye to Christianity."

The concern of my colleagues, as well as the university administration, would be pastoral, that is, how could an unbeliever teach Christianity and Catholicism to impressionable undergraduates (that is, how could the unbeliever be a catechist)? Oddly, the same pastoral concern has kept religious studies departments from hiring Mormons, Catholics and Protestant fundamentalists: how could anyone who believes "that stuff" teach impressionable undergraduates without corrupting them? Prove to us, in other words, how you can belong to a screwy religion and still be one of us.

The Roman Catholic *Mandatum* expresses this, even if only in a minimalist way, so as not to cause the Catholic universities more trouble than their public reputation can bear. The bishops only ask that the theologians not teach something as Catholic doctrine which is not in fact so - as if we would be tempted to abandon our professional ethics as teachers, as if we would teach Milton Friedman economics and call it Catholic social teaching! The bishops recognize, at least as a matter of importance to the universities, that control must be downplayed if academic respect is to be maintained. This is an improvement in the short run, though in the long run the *Mandatum* threatens to resurrect the savagery of the treatment of Charles Curran at Catholic University of America in the 1980s or of the Catholic modernists in the first half of the last century.

In the Curran case, of most unhappy memory, the theologians themselves, at Catholic University and in the professional societies, issued statements that insisted a mistake was being made and that poor Curran "is so" a Catholic theologian, no matter what Cardinal Ratzinger said. But keep in mind that they did not raise a finger other than to write a protest. They did not demand, or picket, or strike. And in the other Catholic universities where Curran's services would putatively have been of high value, the theologians did nothing to provide him with a place and a living. They left the job to the Methodists.

Unlike Loisy for most of his Catholic academic career, Lüdemann is honest. Loisy knew just what the score was and dissimulated for years. In the game of direct control of the universities by the church authorities things are supposed to be significantly different now. The theologians are supposed to police themselves and the university retains "due autonomy." Now the deed can be done in the name of the needs of the mission and identity of the university itself. But the effect is the same: we may silence voices that contradict what we "know" to be true and we thus protect students from corruption. The Church has a hard time wrapping its mind around a theology placed in the university and yet not answerable to the ecclesiastical authorities. In this situation let us hope, and even pray, that Lüdemann, unlike Curran, will not suffer exile in any form. And whatever the event, may he, like Küng, go from grace to grace.

14

Donald Wiebe

University of Toronto

Gerd Lüdemann's "The Decline of Academic Theology at Göttingen" raises significant issues with respect to the legitimacy of theology's place in the curriculum of the modern research university and especially so with respect to the question of academic freedom for the student of religion in that setting. And I am in fundamental agreement with his central contention that any study of religion undertaken in the context of the modern university that is beholden to religious authority, either in respect of its approach to the data or the understanding of religion to which it comes, is unacceptable. However, I am not persuaded by his argument that the University's action in renaming his chair and hiring a new professor of New Testament Studies for the Faculty of Theology amounts to an attack on academic freedom in the University. Nor do I think that this apparent infringement of his academic rights is indicative of a decline in the quality of the "academic theology" at Göttingen, or that the quality of that theological enterprise is on that account necessarily inferior to the work of the earlier Göttingen theologians who formed the History of Religions School, a tradition of scholarship in which he places his own work. Indeed, given the complex nature of the legal issues connected with the Faculty of Theology's existence in the University, I find the arguments and evidence presented by Lüdemann in support of the claim that his academic freedom has been compromised and that he has been unfairly deprived of his academic rights problematic.

I acknowledge, however, that my judgement in this regard is based simply on the information provided by Lüdemann in this very brief paper, and I therefore draw conclusions here somewhat tentatively. Furthermore, it is not simply the lack of information that makes a comprehensive and fully adequate response to Lüdemann's claims in this paper possible. The paper deals with multiple agendas — legal, moral, religious, historical, institutional, and philosophical — which are not clearly delineated, making his comments on these matters of little probative value. And the same may be said of the complex and difficult questions he raises — Are science and religion compatible? Is theology possible in the academy? Is theology a scientific enterprise? Can it ever be? Is a symbolic approach to religious literature religiously inappropriate? (or scientifically inappropriate?) — which for the most part are presented rhetorically, or for which he provides only summary answers, but are nevertheless presumed to present support for his stated positions. In this response to Lüdemann I shall focus primarily on his claims regarding the infringement of his academic rights, but will also comment briefly on the claim — implicit in the title of his paper — that his (symbolic) expulsion from the Faculty of Theology is indicative of a decline in scholarship in the theological project at Göttingen. In conclusion to this "analysis" of Lüdemann's indictments and criticisms of the Faculty and the University, I shall make some brief comments on what I consider his optimistic claims about the possibility of (re)creating a genuine "academic theology" at Göttingen by modelling it on the academic study of religion found in the English-speaking world.

First, then, Lüdemann's indictment that his treatment by the Faculty of Theology and the University amount to an abrogation of academic freedom and an infringement upon his academic rights. Since he has not, technically, been evicted from the Faculty of Theology the exact character of the damage done to him in the dispute with his colleagues and church authorities is difficult to determine. Furthermore, it is no easy matter to adjudicate the dispute because there is a peculiar historical and legal relationship between the church and the state on the place of theology in German universities that appears to exempt that enterprise from the normal regulations governing appointments and responsibilities of members of the teaching staff in theology. As Lüdemann himself notes, "[t]reaties between the state and the Christian churches guarantee the existence of ... theological faculties in Germany," and he acknowledges that these faculties "are responsible for the training not only of future pastors, but also for teachers of religion [i.e. religious educators]" in German schools. He also acknowledges that "[a]nyone who wants to pass a theological examination must be a baptized member of one of the major Christian denominations." and on the basis of these facts it is clear that the education provided by the Faculty of Theology is not simply "scientific" but rather involves the students in preparation for specific professional careers either in or closely related to the church. And this seems to me to imply that it is not only the University but also the Church that has responsibility for the curriculum of the Faculty.

Further, given the requirement of students to be members of one of the major Christian denominations, it seems reasonable that the same requirement would apply to those who teach in the Faculty. Lüdemann maintains that no veto on appointments exist in treaties between the Protestant churches and the state — as is the case in Catholic faculties of theology — but he does not provide an account of what he thinks are the legal implications of that fact. Moreover, his reference to the reintroduction in 1995 of an oath of 1848 requiring "agreement with the principles of the Evangelical Lutheran Church" is ambiguous and suggests that perhaps the "baptism" requirement for professors might have been legally in force throughout the period from 1848 to 1995, even if not strictly enforced. Given the ambiguity of these matters and the concomitant uncertainty as to the full meaning of the treaty between church and state involving the University of Göttingen, it would have been helpful in understanding his situation had Lüdemann provided some elaboration of and response to the expert legal opinion of the lawyers for the Confederation of Lutheran Churches in Lower Saxony that, as he admits, "argues that the University *must* transfer [him] to another faculty." Lüdemann obviously believes that any connection between theology and the church is indicative of an "epistemic failure" in the theological project at Göttingen — that is, that it involves "academic theology" in a sort of methodological contradiction and that it ought not therefore to be legitimated by the academic community — but this is irrelevant to the legal issues connected to the Church's historical treaty rights, and Lüdemann, I think, fails to provide sufficient warrant for his charges against the University.

In light of the admitted "legal status of theological faculties in Germany", it is difficult to see why Lüdemann objects to the "interim" resolution of the dispute reached by the University, the Confederation of Lutheran Churches in Lower Saxony, and the Ministry of Science and Culture that involved his chair being renamed "History and Literature of Early Christianity." Further, one might reasonably have expected Lüdemann's identification with the work of the History of Religions School in the Faculty of Theology at Göttingen at the end of the nineteenth and the beginning of the twentieth century sufficient reason for him to accept the "realignment of chairs and duties" as more academically acceptable than remaining professor of New Testament studies. He admits that the change guarantees him the academic freedom required for the unity of research and teaching that is of the essence of the modern university, yet nevertheless still claims that he has been denied his *academic rights.* Insofar as this decision voids his old contract with the University of Göttingen, and, according to Lüdemann, reduces his research funds, as well as his access to a research assistant, and, presuming that those perquisites were contractually tied to his former chair, he appears to have a justifiable academic grievance. He may also have grounds for concern for the careers of his doctoral students, although he has provided no evidence to support a claim that his graduate students have been negatively affected by this change, or that these changes amount to a loss of academic freedom for him.

I am therefore not persuaded by the argument presented here that Lüdemann has been denied *academic rights* connected to his "old discipline," unless, of course, Lüdemann means by this the fact that he has been removed from the *training* of pastors and teachers of Protestant religion in the public school system. But this would be odd given that Lüdemann has rejected the Christian faith. Nevertheless, it appears that he does believe that his removal from such a task is a loss of academic freedom for he asserts that "the result of these [University] actions is that no students attend my classes [and] the academic theological guild in Germany avoids me..." I take this to mean not that the University prevents Lüdemann from offering courses, or students from taking them, but rather that the religious authorities will not grant theological students credit in the area of New Testament studies for courses taken with Lüdemann who is now in the "area" of "History and Literature of Early Christianity." However, it may be the case that Lüdemann believes that he has lost his academic rights because in being removed from the Faculty of Theology he has been stripped of any role in the shaping of the theological enterprise in the future. For example, he protests that there is no guarantee that any curriculum he might create in his new discipline will be continued in the Faculty, and he complains that he will not likely be replaced in the Faculty upon his retirement in 2011.

But these concerns, surely, are not matters indissolubly connected to the question of academic freedom; nor are they, so far as I can see, a loss of academic rights. If the issue here is that Lüdemann must be allowed to teach required classes to students who are baptized members of the church preparing for church ministry or for providing religious education in the public school system his complaint, in light of the treaties that apparently guarantee the church jurisdiction over the teaching of theology in the University, seems to me to be without warrant. Similarly problematic is Lüdemann's apparent claim that it is his academic right not only to present the conclusions of his scientific research in New Testament studies but also that he be allowed to press for a restructuring of the Faculty of Theology on the basis of his (ir)religious conclusions "grounded," according to him, in his scientific research. Odd as this may be, it seems to be the position he holds, for, as he puts it, "[a]s long as theology remains in the university, it has to research and inform, not reveal and preach; to bring people to maturity in matters of religion, not lead them astray into servitude to an old superstition, no matter how modern it may claim to be." To do otherwise, he asserts, is to undermine the academic character of the theological enterprise by the *a priori* adoption of a faith position. Hence his views must be accepted by the church in preference to the views of his colleagues who, he claims, "attach themselves to this tradition by symbolic and other [illicit] interpretative skills."

It is clear, then, that Lüdemann not only consciously contradicts the position of the church but believes it his academic right to force the church to subordinate its religious mission to the purely scientific agenda of the University to which he is now committed. The church, however, does not concur with that judgement, nor need it do so given its historic treaty with the state. That treaty, it appears, has in effect created a kind of independent seminary status for the Faculty of Theology within the university framework that exempts it from the ordinary cognitive and disciplinary standards governing other university enterprises. Nor do Lüdemann's colleagues agree that the enterprise they are engaged in is a purely scientific one, and it is perhaps a bit unfair for Lüdemann to dismiss so summarily their symbolic and interpretative skills as illicit or merely measures adopted for the sake of expediency. And Lüdemann's laudatory comments about the scientific nature of the project of those involved in the "History of Religions School" in the past do not provide incontrovertible evidence that recourse to symbolic and hermeneutical devices in the theological enterprise is a recent invention of the members of the Faculty of Theology. He does not show, that is, that his predecessors in that School differed greatly with respect to liberal Christian commitments from his contemporary colleagues in the Faculty. Did all his *Religionsgeschichtliche Schule* predecessors consider their scientific research a falsification of "Christian faith"? The answer, clearly, is no.

Looked at critically, I am not altogether sure that Lüdemann's desire to remain in the Faculty of Theology, but not as a Christian professor, might not justifiably be taken to amount to a kind of crypto-religious rather than a strictly scientific agenda. In response to the charge by his colleagues that his desire to remain in the Faculty of Theology is disingenuous he writes: "This decision is based on my firm intention to bring to bear the best traditions of free Protestant theology and to reestablish the critical principle within the confessional faculties which have become so compliant as to be anaemic." This might well suggest that Lüdemann is still somehow engaged in the same enterprise as they; that is, that he is still engaged, although in a more scientific manner, in religious discourse. If in the best traditions of free Protestant theology they must leave open the possibility that scientific claims might undermine judgements of faith, he would, according to those same principles, be obliged to leave open the possibility that even though *current scientific claims* might clash with *contemporary formulations of faith*, a compatibility system harmonizing the two sets of assertions might well be possible in the future. But in the Weberian terms espoused by Lüdemann, even this kind of theological stance involves the sacrifice of intellect that Lüdemann claims no scientist can espouse. Clearly, then, Lüdemann has given up not only Christian faith but all religious faith and therefore does not leave open the "possibility" of ever achieving a compatibility system that will harmonize science and religion. His claim, therefore, that he is working within a revitalized Protestant framework is less than convincing.

I turn now to Lüdemann's charge that the attempt to evict him from the Faculty of Theology is indicative of a decline in the quality of the theological enterprise at Göttingen. The title of his paper, I suggest, indicates that Lüdemann here trades on an ambiguous use of the word "theology." Lüdemann, that is, uses the word to cover both the "capital-C" confessional theology (based on revelation of divine Truth and embodied in creedal statements) done in the Faculty of Theology as distinct from what goes on in other academic pursuits at Göttingen and the "academic/scientific study of religion" that he acknowledges is carried out in social science departments and elsewhere in the University. His argument is further weakened, moreover, in that he suggests, but does not show, that the kind of "academic theology" that amounts to "religious studies" ever existed at Göttingen. He provides no evidence, for example, that his forebears in the Faculty who formed the History of Religions School — in which tradition of scholarship he considers himself to be functioning — conceived of their work as "religious studies" in the sense in which he uses that term here. Nor does he establish the implicit claim in his discussion of this group of Protestant theologians that they were driven to public repudiation of their religious commitments on the basis of their scientific findings. It is not clear, therefore, that the History of Religions School achieved in their scholarship the bench mark of "the scientific study of religion" to which Lüdemann is committed and from which his contemporary colleagues, according to him, have fallen. Indeed, their work was very much a religious enterprise and not a purely academic one.

In lodging this criticism against Lüdemann's central argument, however, I mean to suggest neither that theology is a scientific discipline nor that it ought still today to have a place in the academy alongside other *bona fide* scientific enterprises. The primary purpose of the modern research university, as Edward Shils points out, is to obtain rationally and empirically sound knowledge of the world and to make it available for the management of the affairs of society. And, as Lüdemann has correctly pointed out, that is not the primary focus of the theological enterprise. It is clear, therefore, that the existence of theological faculties in the German universities is academically anomalous even though legally sanctioned. As Shils puts it in his discussion of academic freedom, it exists in the modern university with the exception of the *modus vivendi* reached in German universities which, although they excluded the churches from any direct or constitutional influence on the universities that could undermine their cognitive objectives, they permitted "a small qualification regarding [academic freedom and] chairs of theology' (285). Whether that "arrangement" ought still to continue, however, is another matter, and on this issue I am in entire agreement with Lüdemann. Although one can understand the reasons that led to this peculiar political arrangement, it is clear that in the, paradoxically, secular and multi-religious nature of German society today this *academic* anomaly in the university is no longer *politically* justifiable.

Finally, some brief comments on Lüdemann's proposal to stem the decline in the academic theological enterprise in the University of Göttingen by constructing a truly "scientific theology," a phrase he uses to designate an "honest and unblinking examination of religion." Lüdemann, unfortunately, creates considerable confusion in presenting his proposal by a somewhat sloppy use of terminology. He seems to equate "academic theology" not only with the contemporary theological enterprise at Göttingen to which he objects, but also with an acceptable "scientific theology" which he in turn uncritically identifies with "the academic study of religion." He is fully aware that the kind of academic study of religion in which he wishes to engage, but cannot, in the Faculty of Theology as presently constituted — that is, a purely scientific study of religions — is undertaken in other (historical and social-scientific) disciplines within in German universities, but he laments the lack of the kind of departmental institutionalisation of the purely scientific study of religion in German universities that "one finds in the English-speaking world and in other parts of Europe." He writes: "Despite the pretenses of the confessional theologians, a religious studies program offering genuine breadth of scope, solid scholarly foundations, and true academic freedom is to all intents and purposes practically non-existent in German universities." However, it appears that Lüdemann also believes that the Faculty of Theology, because it exists within the framework and under the auspices of the university, ought to fill that role in German universities and, perhaps, even that it did so in the past.

But as I have already indicated above, Lüdemann's historical argument with respect to the History of Religions School is unpersuasive, and his structural argument is without forces since, legally speaking, the Faculty of Theology need not provide the ethos necessary for establishing a genuinely scientific study of religion. I think, therefore, Lüdemann could provide a much stronger argument for the institutionalisation of the scientific study of religion within the academy were he to let go of "theology" altogether, including what he calls "scientific theology," and stick to the nomenclature of "religious studies" for the peculiar academic enterprise he has in mind. Whatever the pretenses of the theologians to whom Lüdemann refers, the faculties of theology established by treaty between church and state in Germany are not, and were never intended to be, departments of Religious Studies, committed to working wholly within a naturalistic framework with the aim of finding a natural (explanatory, theoretical) account of religion. Therefore the response to Lüdemann's question Does theology which is in the service of the church/synagogue/mosque belong in the universities at all? the answer must be both "yes" and "no." By treaty/law theology in the service of the church (not synagogue or mosque) has a right to exist in the *German* university, although in terms of the essential cognitive function filled by the modern university it ought not to have that "legitimation" given the intrinsic contradiction such theology exhibits in claiming for itself scientific status for its understanding of religions and religion while also claiming that the results of its research must be consistent with the dogmas of the church. This explains my judgement that Lüdemann is without justification in the claim that his academic freedom and rights have been breached by the realignment of chairs and duties fashioned by the University and the Ministry of Science and Culture. I do not believe, that is, that in trying to prevent Lüdemann from effecting a transformation of the Faculty of Theology into a department of Religious Studies — which it appears is his goal — infringes upon his academic freedoms; but it does allow him to continue to treat religion "as an evolving phenomenon subject to human history" as does the academic study of religion. As I have already noted, I believe Lüdemann to be right in his claim that confessional (capital-C or small-c) theology does not belong in the curriculum of the modern research university, and I support his bid to institutionalise the scientific study of religion at Göttingen, but I believe him to be without academic, legal, or moral justification in attempting to achieve this end through a forced transformation of its Faculty of Theology. I am simply not persuaded by his assumption that the claim of the Faculty to be engaging in "scientific theology" is an implicit acknowledgment that it is engaged in "religious studies."

In summary, then, I would have no quarrel with Lüdemann were he to argue that the current treaties between church and state that provide an exceptional role for theology in the context of the university ought to be revoked; nor would I find fault with a call for the University to consider support for the creation of a separate department for the scientific study of religion and religions subject to the same constraints that apply to all scientific endeavours in the university. Lüdemann's appeal to Weber here is entirely on the mark — theology of any kind demands sacrifice of the intellect because it must presuppose revelation. I am a little sceptical, however, about his rather rosy view of the "academic study of religion" in the English-speaking world as a quintessentially scientific enterprise. Unfortunate though it may be, much of the scholarship in that "framework" is not really free from theology, even though it may not be governed by a capital-C Confessionalism that presumes the creeds are based upon divinely revealed truths, much of it nevertheless does espouse a small-c confessionalism in (intuitively) assuming that religions ultimately relate to Transcendent Reality. However, unlike most scholars in departments of Theology, many in departments of Religious Studies at least claim to be engaged in an academic pursuit indistinguishable in structure and aim from other disciplines in the university. Nevertheless, attempting to establish a purely scientific agenda in the field of Religious Studies today is still an incredibly difficult undertaking and progress has been slow; attempting to do that in the context of a Faculty of Theology beholden to the church is, in my opinion, both inappropriate and impossible.

15

Response

by Gerd Lüdemann

My concluding remarks afford me the opportunity first to comment on the articles by Professors Presser, Shea and Wiebe which argue against my remaining in the theological faculty (Presser, Shea) or dispute my claim to be seriously deprived of academic rights (Wiebe), and second to correct some factual misrepresentations by Dean Kratz. In my reply to the latter, I shall not dispute him on juridical and theological grounds, but will attempt to set the record straight so that on the basis of his statement and my introductory essay readers may be enabled to draw their own conclusions.

As Professor Presser is surely aware, believing that God exists and believing that the law serves the interests of justice are very different from "believing in the river" – whatever that may be taken to mean. The steamboat pilot is committed not to the river, but to successfully *navigating* the river. Any argument based on such a faulty analogy as Presser advances is seriously flawed from the start. Furthermore, as Twain makes very clear, the reason every boy dreamed of being a pilot was the wonderful payoff in money and esteem. The pilot received a princely salary and was viewed as a superior person. He gave orders to everyone and took orders from no one. He was, within his limited domain, an absolute authority. Of course, he was subject to the objective evaluation of the river: if he wrecked the boat on a rock or got it stuck on a sandbar, his error was obvious and beyond doubt. One could wish that lawyers and clergy were subject to similar evaluations of their work. It might change their tune a bit. Instead, they rally around one another and assure us that the system is working well (in the case of the clergy, despite the fact of a continuing diminution in church attendance and general disaffection with matters religious). Indeed, those who point out the flaws in Christianity as it is presently constituted may well provide it a more useful service than those defenders who cannot or will not see the snags and dangerous currents in the river ahead.

Presser, like so many of his colleagues from German law schools, fails to recognize that Western culture is today challenging much of the theology that is its heritage, simply because that theology has been outdated by the universally shared modern understanding of the world. Surely schools of theology should be fully prepared to deal constructively with this well-attested fact.

As concerns Professor Shea, although he is a committed and concerned "insider" who is clearly "playing it safe", he is at least forthright and magnanimous in confessing his admiration for someone who has the courage to take great personal and professional risks in the interests of truth. Still, reading his critique, one wonders a little about his own *ultimate commitment and concern* (a phrase which is often employed as a synonym for God). Is it to truth, or is it to the university and church – institutions which furnish him with a paycheck and a gratifying degree of status?

Moreover, as Shea must know full well, one is increasingly obliged to deal seriously with the question of whether it is necessary to affirm the traditional Christian doctrines in order consider oneself a Christian. The examples of Bishop John Shelby Spong and Lloyd Geering and a majority of the scholars of the Jesus Seminar suggest that it is not. Indeed, among serious Christian scholars the definitions of "God" and "Christianity" are presently in such a state of flux that it is doubtful whether anyone can offer generally satisfactory definitions for either.

In such a context prospective clergymen have a crying need for teachers who will present serious and responsible challenges to traditional belief systems. The great English Puritan John Milton, in his famous essay *Aereopagitica* correctly decried " a fugitive and cloistered virtue, unexercised and unbreathed, that never sallies out and sees her adversary, but slinks out of the race ..."

I am puzzled by a number of Professor Donald Wiebe's comments. For example, in his opening paragraph he agrees that it is unacceptable for university studies to be under the control of religious authorities, and then offers what is surely a conflicting opinion concerning my case: that when the University – at the behest of religious authorities – took actions which have marginalized my position and restricted my ability to perform the scholarly and instructional functions essential to my professorship, those actions affected neither my academic freedom nor the quality of the University's educational offering.

It also seems strange that Prof. Wiebe should express uncertainty as to the extent of the damage done to my role as an instructor, to say nothing of the opportunity to carry out my own research and to foster the investigations of others. For only two pages later he lists several specific constraints that were imposed, and asserts that I have "a justifiable academic grievance." Let me hasten to add that all of my graduate students have been affected the consequence of which is, if they still want to pursue a doctorate, they have to deny their association with me and/or have to look for another doctoral father. I thought a contract remains valid. Yet I had to find out that even a respected University can break a contract and then claim that everything is O.K. because of the previous change of the name of my chair.

Needless to say I based future careers of promising scholars on such an arrangement but was mistaken.

It is gratifying that Wiebe is able to draw the conclusion that the church shares with the University responsibility for the curriculum; yet it is strange that having in the introductory paragraph termed this an unacceptable state of affairs, he now finds nothing particularly wrong with the situation. Indeed, he deems the requirement for church membership "reasonable" and "the Church's historical treaty rights" unassailable. Worse yet, the treaty relationship he finds so important involves the State and the University in joining the Church in the presupposition of revealed truths that are of a higher order than discovered truths. Perhaps it is at precisely this point that we should recognize the true locus of the present conflict, and understand that it is time to begin the difficult task of revising the legal and procedural relations between the Church, the State, and the University.

In other words, it is not simply or even primarily a matter of my professional or personal prerogatives, but removing undue hindrances from the free operation of investigation and the untrammeled pursuit of knowledge.

At the end of his fifth paragraph Wiebe finds – as I noted earlier – that I have "a justifiable academic grievance," but he opens the very next paragraph with the opinion that I have not been denied any academic rights connected to my chair in theology.

I think it is fair to put the following key question: Should an internationally known and respected New Testament scholar be barred from teaching church members who are preparing to become clergy or teachers of religion on the sole grounds that he is not himself a believing Christian? In other words, is his or her analysis of Scripture and the reconstruction of early Christian history though being identical in the time before and after the departure from the Christian religion theologically less valuable one day after having renounced Christianity? Wiebe obviously thinks so, and considers any claim by such a person to exercise such a right as an invalid presumption. Does he fear that the university experience will result in the contamination of the faithful by divergent opinions? Would he prefer teachers of lesser academic stature but greater orthodoxy of belief – or perhaps those who would hypocritically dissemble or remain silent to protect their positions?

Wiebe is flagrantly in error (end of par. 7) when he ascribes to me the opinion that my view must be accepted by the church. Furthermore, this simply does not follow – as he proposes it does – from my belief that the job of the university is "to research and inform, not to reveal and preach." Unless, that is, he has fixed in his mind the notion that the treaty relationship between the Church and the University has made them for all intents and purposes one and the same institution.

He further errs when he says afterwards that I believe it to be my right "to force the church to subordinate its religious mission to the purely scientific agenda of the University." I have no such right, of course, nor do I seek it or anything like it. To be sure, it might be a salutary thing for churches to become a little less insistent on outmoded claims of revelation and a little more open to the conventional world view of the twenty-first century – but that is another matter.

Nor do I suggest, as he claims, that the scholars of the History of Religions School saw their work as a "falsification of the 'Christian faith'." A challenge to certain doubtful doctrines hardly amounts to the falsification of a faith. Yet he should have known better that indeed some of the members of the History of Religions School in Göttingen (e.g. Wilhelm Bousset, Heinrich Hackmann, Ernst Troeltsch) and sympathizers elsewhere (e.g. Franz Overbeck, Carl Albrecht Bernoulli, Gustav Krüger) conceived (at least part of) their studies as tantamount to Religious Studies today or Scientific Theology as I would prefer to call it.

Wiebe is also wrong (par.9) in ascribing to me a "crypto-religious... agenda," whatever that means; and is not only incorrect, but presumptuous when he claims I have given up all religious faith and have shut the door on "any system that will harmonize science and religion." How can he make such statements about someone he does not know?

One is again confused by the repeated assertions in paragraph 11 that the study of theology has become a no longer justifiable anomaly in the University, when in a subsequent paragraph (13) he says that it both does and does not belong there: it doesn't by rights, but it does by law. And therefore, he concludes, no abrogation of my rights or academic freedom has taken place. By what is essentially the same argument, slaves, ethnic and religious minorities, and women have been and continue to be kept in their places. One suspects that Wiebe is what the Americans call "a company man": he wouldn't try to change the existing rules of the firm no matter what principle might be defended or what benefit realized.

He admits in his closing paragraph that to establish an academically respectable department "in the field of religious studies today is an incredibly difficult undertaking, and progress has been slow ..." True, but as he notes, any progress lies in that direction. It is therefore most puzzling that his very last statement is that "... attempting to do that in the context of a Faculty of Theology beholden to the church is ... both inappropriate and impossible."

One could properly ask for a bit more consistency and accuracy in so acidulous a critique. And anyway, what are we really arguing about, Professor Wiebe? It seems to boil down to departmental titles and the political status quo.

Concerning the statement of Dean Kratz, I feel compelled to correct several inaccurate assertions:

a) It is untrue to say that I could no longer fill my previous position in the New Testament faculty in full accord with my conscience and my convictions. My spiritual home remains the free Protestantism (like that of Albert Schweitzer) which does not subscribe to dogmas, but which traditionally belongs to protestant theological faculties.

b) It is untrue to say that I had taught freely before the Confederation of Evangelical Churches officially asked the government to remove me from my position. Rather, as a result of my criticizing the church's practice of ordination, I was removed in 1996 from the examining board of the Protestant Churches in Lower Saxony; and subsequent to the publication of my book "The Resurrection of Jesus" (1994), I was repeatedly the target of denunciations by the Bishop of Hannover. (For example, he wrote about me: "This man wants to be scourged.")

c) It is untrue to say that since 1998 my freedom of research has not been curtailed. To my way of thinking, taking away the post of an assistant corresponding to an Assistant Professor and cutting research money in half – neither of which in my case has anything to do with a five year period – amount to a serious impediment of free research because they do not allow me to carry out scholarly inquiries I had planned.

d) It is untrue to ascribe to me the view that the teaching of theology at German institutions of higher learning does not meet acceptable academic standards. All I have claimed is that the pursuit of theology as an academic discipline should not be tied to the confession of the church, and that if it is, it is not a true academic discipline.

e) It is misleading to say that I have the unrestricted right to hold examinations in the field of "History and Literature of Early Christianity". First, no such program of studies exists at my University. Second, given the attitude of the theological and philosophical faculties, should I submit a curriculum, its academic status would be uncertain – to say nothing of the fact that it would be a one-man program and would be abolished upon my retirement in 2011.

f) It is untrue to say that I originally accepted the "settlement" of the President of my University. This report was orally transmitted to the Dean by a non-academic legal counsel of the University at a time when the details of such a "settlement" were not even worked out. I did agree to a renaming of my chair because the New Testament consists of the literature of Early Christianity and presupposes its history. Yet I insisted on examining rights within the theological faculty for students who would not become pastors.

g) Let me hasten to add that up to the present day "the settlement" remains preliminary, and has not been finally accepted by the Confederation of Protestant Churches in Lower Saxony.

Last of all, given the facts of the case, the dean's statement that I had a change of mind and retracted an agreement, combined with his insinuation that my actions have been arbitrary and frivolous, amount to an unwarranted attack on my character. *Satis sit.*

16

This Theology Is Not an Academic Discipline

A Plea for Faculties
Which Pursue Research into all Religions

Gerd Lüdemann

Frankfurter Rundschau: 4 December 1998

At the beginning of March 1998, as a professor of New Testament on a state faculty, I declared publicly that I was no longer a Christian. Thereupon, several church organizations as well as groups lacking any ecclesiastical affiliation suggested to me that I should transfer to the philosophy faculty and thus make room for a successor who was a believer. I refused to do this, because my analysis of the New Testament still follows the same scholarly criteria and because in Germany the theological faculties have traditionally been places for scholarly research into Christianity. Since this refusal I have increasingly become the target of church sanctions, and now even my own colleagues are calling unanimously for me to be transferred to another faculty, in spite of the state's establishment of an additional parallel chair in New Testament. The decision now lies with the president of Göttingen University.

The events I have described are unique in German Protestantism. They nurture the suspicion that the theology being done in Germany is not an academic discipline at all. Clearly, it cannot be, because it is governed by a confessional approach. In view of this patent contradiction, in view of the dramatic decrease in church attendance and the declining place of Christianity in culture and education, and perhaps especially in view of the seemingly exotic claim of Christian doctrine that Jesus as God's Son suffered for the sins of the world, thereafter to rise incorrupt – in view of all these it is the more puzzling that the theological faculties, ironically divided into Protestant and Catholic branches, are still thought to be an indispensable element of the German university.

The reunification of Germany has not led to any far-reaching changes in this untenable situation, which is based on agreements between the two dominant churches and the state. Like the GDR government previously, the several state governments have in principle respected the existence of state theological faculties, and recently have made generous agreements with the churches — even though in the new federal states only about one third of the population belongs to a church. This support for theology as a discipline is unparalleled anywhere else in the world, especially in its financial aspect, and can be explained only by the long-standing influence of the church. But that is no help: as the following remarks show, the very foundations of present-day academic theology are crumbling.

Most academic theologians begin with two presuppositions. First, theology is a discipline related to the Bible perceived as the word of God. Second, theology assumes the truth-claim of Christian talk of God. Given these axioms, does theology deserve to be called a scholarly discipline?

Since both assumptions are articles of faith, which on critical investigation prove to be empty, the question must be answered with a firm negative. First of all, the Bible is the word of man, and second, it contains a considerable number of different images of God. From a purely scholarly perspective one must ask which God people are to agree on. When the issue comes down to truth claims, the theologian may argue from faith and with greater insight. But that has nothing to do with scholarship; we must not confuse the lecturer's desk and the pulpit.

Furthermore, no one can accede a professorial chair in the German theological faculties without a baptismal certificate and the assent of the respective churches: a Jew cannot be called to a chair in the theological faculties or even gain the necessary qualifications; being unbaptized, he or she can neither take the qualifying examination nor earn a doctorate by scholarly work on the Jew Jesus. The status of the faculties may be guaranteed by law, but sooner or later the anomalous situation will call for changes in legal protocols, and a radical transformation of the existing theological faculty will necessarily result. There are two reasons why this will happen.

The **first** is purely academic: theologians of the two Christian confessions approach texts in the same way, employing philology, historical criticism and comparative religion.

The **second** is a matter of social policy. In the next few years Germany will increasingly become the homeland of members of other religions. If one follows the legalistic logic, these religious communities, as public corporations, likewise deserve to have their own theological faculties. In that case, in the future we would have not only Protestant and Catholic, but also Muslim, Jewish and Buddhist faculties — perhaps even faculties of Jehovah's Witnesses and Mormons. It must be clear to everyone that this would be not only financially impossible, but in terms of scholarship as anachronistic as the present Christian faculties. For scholarly research into Christian, Muslim, or Buddhist faith can no more be Christian, Muslim, or Buddhist than criminology can be criminal. Science and scholarship eschew presuppositions and recognize a duty to objective truthfulness.

In this matter, the present situation in German theology is unhealthy, if only on legal grounds. By law, the Roman Catholic Church can block the appointment of disapproved lecturers, and even exclude candidates it deems undesirable. And now, in my case, the Protestant Church has claimed the same right for itself.

The need to transform the theological faculties can be seen also in the increasing unification of Europe. The German situation is unique, and in the long term cannot survive in the European Community. In other European countries, as in North America, people are following the discussion in Germany – once the Mecca of scholarly theology — with amazement and dismay. The clear and present remedy is for far-sighted politicians to prune back the dead branches and permit scholarship to bear its appropriate fruit.

The requirement of the hour is a new faculty of theology or religious studies, one which delves into all religions of the past and present. This faculty would include members of the traditional Protestant and Catholic faculties — in considerably reduced numbers — along with the occupants of chairs in the history of religion, religious studies, and, where appropriate, philosophy. The practical and doctrinal training of clergy is the task of the Christian churches and other religious communities; it is not the business of the university.

(Translated from the German by Dr. John Bowden and edited by Tom Hall)

17

Reply from the Theological Faculty of the University of Rostock

Lüdemann ist das genaue Spiegelbild, das er beschwört

Prof. Dr. Eckart Reinmuth für das Kollegium der Theol. Fakultät Rostock

Frankfurter Rundschau 7. Januar 1999

Zum Gastbeitrag Diese Theologie ist keine Wissenschaft (Frankfurter Rundschau vom 4. Dezember 1998) von Gerd Lüdemann:
Die akademische Auseinandersetzung mit den Thesen Gerd Lüdemanns ist nicht auf den Seiten einer Tageszeitung zu führen. Die öffentliche Diskriminierung der wissenschaftlichen Theologie indessen darf gerade hier nicht unwidersprochen bleiben.

Welches auch immer die persönlichen Motive unseres Göttinger Kollegen sein mögen—er verbreitet entgegen dem ihm zu Gebote stehenden Wissen gezielt Unwahrheiten. Die lieblose Formulierung, es sei zentraler Glaubensinhalt, daß Gottes Sohn in der Gestalt Jesu für die Sünden dieser Welt büßte, um anschließend unverweslich aufzuerstehen, ist eine öffentliche Irreführung, die mit Hilfe einer sinnlosen Collage aus scheinbar dogmatischen Versatzstücken zeigen soll, wie unzeitgemäß die Aufgabenstellung christlicher Theologie sei.

Lüdemann weiß genau, daß theologische Forschung und Lehre von anderen Voraussetzungen bestimmt sind, und er weiß auch um die Vielfalt interdisziplinärer Zusammenarbeit, die kaum möglich wäre, wenn seine

Behauptungen zuträfen. Aber er weigert sich—die Wissenschaft auf seiner Seite wähnend—grundlegende Einsichten historisch-kritischen Denkens, also eines sachgemäßen Umgangs mit Literatur und Geschichte, zu realisieren. Sein trotziger Positivismus befindet sich außerhalb dessen, was gegenwärtig als geistes- und kulturwissenschaftlicher Konsens gilt. Wir werden uns nicht verständigen können. Wer so die Öffentlichkeit veralbert, wünscht die Rolle, die er beklagt. Aber offenbar handelt es sich um handfeste Interessen in diesem Streit.

Wieder werden bewußt Vorurteile aktiviert, obwohl man es besser weiß. Wieder wird mit aufgeklärtem Pathos verkündet, daß die Bibel Menschenwort sei und eine Vielzahl von Gottesbildern enthalte—wer soll mit solchen Gemeinplätzen verschaukelt werden?

Hier wird gerade nicht aufgeklärt, wie es die Pflicht der Theologie wäre, sondern Unkenntnis mutwillig befördert. Es zeichnet aber dies die christliche Theologie aus, daß sie kritische Partnerin eines Glaubens ist, der nicht ohne sie sein kann.

Der Streit um das leere Grab spielt für die neutestamentliche Theologie ungefähr die gleiche Rolle, wie wenn ich sage—"ich liebe dich", und will dies mit einem vor Jahren geschenkten Blumenstrauß beweisen. Aber das Verwirrspiel mit den Beweisen ist vorbei, und die Zeiten sind ebenfalls vorbei, in denen die emanzipatorische Arbeit der Theologie sich an den Popanzen konstruierter Fragestellungen abarbeiten durfte, die nur verhindern sollen, die richtigen fragen zu stellen. Denn das "ich liebe dich" bleibt aus, wenn die Theologie sich weigert, diese Worte zu buchstabieren, sondern ihr Gezänk darüber wiederholt, wie das mit dem einstigen Blumenstrauß gewesen ist.

Gerade da, wo es Theologen wie Lüdemann nicht gelingt, zwischen den wissenschaftlichen Grundlagen ihrer Disziplin und den Konstitutionsbedingungen der Moderne zu unterscheiden, fällt die Entdeckung ihrer Fraglichkeit auf die Theologie zurück. Lüdemann ist das genaue Zerrbild der Theologie, das er beschwört.

Er bekämpft verbliebene Ruinen, weil ihm offenbar die Herausforderung, vor der Theologie (und Kirchen!) tatsächlich stehen, unheimlich sind. Es geht doch um nicht weniger als die bleibende Aufgabe, im Konzert der Weltdeutungen die Stimme verständlich zu Gehör zu bringen, die sich dem Anstoß des Mannes aus Galiläa verdankt.

18

Whither Theology?

Either a discipline free of the church or no scholarly discipline at all

Gerd Lüdemann

Frankfurter Rundschau: 16 April 1999

We cannot envisage the disappearance of theological and ecclesiastical concerns from government. They have a solid backing, even in disturbed times when purse strings are tight. In Germany the churches, as public corporations, levy upon their members taxes which are collected by the state; and theological faculties are protected by agreements between the state and the churches. The Basic Law (Article 7, para.3) provides for offering religious education 'in accord with the basic principles of the religious communities'. And to be sure, theological studies have been part of the canon of disciplines since the foundation of the European universities in the thirteenth century. But things are beginning to change. We are presently witnessing a slow but sure decline in the popular acceptance, and indeed the very plausibility of many traditional Christian doctrines, and both with the public and within the university, theology is increasingly losing credit as an academic discipline, let alone a study to be funded by the state.

Yet Protestant theology in particular has an impressive achievement to point to, and has been an important element of German intellectual history. At the beginning of this century Albert Schweitzer summed up its significance this way: 'When, at some future day, our period of civilization lies closed and completed before the eyes of later generations, German theology will stand as a great, a unique phenomenon in the mental and spiritual life of our time.' In this remark Schweitzer was referring first to the honest and objective investigation of the sources of the Christian faith appearing in the Old and New Testaments, and second, he had in view the attempts made by every new generation to relate the message of the Bible truthfully to the current world.

We may add that scholarly theology practised in this way from German professorial chairs set the standard for theological faculties throughout the world, and at least until the middle of the twentieth century German was the language of international theology. What is the basis of the power of a theology practised in this way?

First, its approach consists in making a radical historical investigation of its own religion. That commonly leads to many results which are diametrically opposed to statements in the Bible. Thus Jesus was not born of a virgin, he neither desired nor intended to die for the sins of humankind, and he certainly did not rise bodily from the tomb as the Gospels report.

Second, by means of objective comparisons it examines congruities between early Christianity and other religions contemporaneous with it. Contrary to the claim of the biblical authors, that tends to lead to a relativizing of Christian faith; for almost all the teachings of Jesus – from the injunction to love one's neighbor to the insinuations of the parables – can be found in the Judaism of his time; and countless parallels outside the early church correspond to what the New Testament calls 'faith'.

Third, sociological and psychological issues have become inherent parts of theological investigation, for they afford us a better understanding of early Christian communities and the persons active in them. Here again, however, we find manifest discrepancies with the scriptural accounts. When the Bible talks of the community and individuals 'being filled with the Holy Spirit', in reality it describes a mass hallucinatory phenomenon or the visionary experience of a highly excitable individual. In every case these represent intrinsically human psychic events, and not supernatural inspiration, as church dogma still declares.

In short, while scholarly theology generally relativizes the truth-claims of the Christian churches, German youth who aspire to lead these churches look to the state theological faculties for their academic training. The resulting conflict runs like a scarlet thread through the history of the theology of the last two centuries. Today, the dominant strain of theology resolves the problem by defining itself as a church discipline. The validity of a theology is thus measured by the degree to which it serves the interests of the church. Professors of theology seek to blunt the penetrating criticism of scholarly methods by making necklaces out of bent spear points. That may be charming, but it is irresponsible. Scholarship strives for objectivity, and precisely for that reason may never predicate the truth-claims of the churches. Theology cannot be a church discipline; either it is a free discipline or it is not a scholarly discipline at all.

The changed social situation similarly demands that theology may no longer understand itself as part of the clerical domain, but rather as an endeavor generally responsible for religion in the contemporary culture. Therefore its task is not solely the academic training of future pastors and teachers of religion it must also offer an introduction and an explanation to all those professions involving religious concerns: social workers, journalists, politicians, and funeral directors – but always as religious studies from the lectern, never as confessional matters from the pulpit.

As long as the churches are closely affiliated with the state and have a share in the culture of the present, there is every reason for their future pastors to continue to receive their academic training from the theological faculty. They will thus receive the preliminary knowledge necessary for an understanding of the Christian faith. Their professional training would then follow, when they must learn to put into practice their churches' belief in the Son of God, whose kingdom, as they themselves preach, is not of this world. Academic theology has its feet firmly planted on this earth where, financed by the secular state, it investigates and teaches religion as a function of the human spirit. If it is to mature and develop, it must unconditionally accept the precept of the English philosopher Bertrand Russell who offered this reassurance: 'Even if the open window of science at first makes us shiver with cold after the cosy indoor warmth of traditional humanizing myths, in the end the fresh air brings vigour, and the great spaces have a splendour of their own.'

(Translated from the German by Dr. John Bowden and edited by Tom Hall)

19

Kirche der Scheinheiligen

Gespräch mit dem Bibelforscher Gerd Lüdemann

EVANGELISCHE KOMMENTARE 3/1999.

Professor Dr. Gerd Lüdemann (52) unterrichtet an der Georg-August-Universität Göttingen das Fach "Geschichte und Literatur des frühen Christentums". Bekannt geworden ist er durch seine Kritik an der Kirche. Seiner Auffassung nach verpflichtet sie ihre Pastoren auf Bekenntnisse, die sich wissenschaftlich nicht mehr halten lassen.

Evangelische Kommentare: Herr Professor Lüdemann, im vergangenen Jahr haben Sie sich vom christlichen Glauben losgesagt. Sie bezeichnen sich öffentlich als Nicht-Christ. Haben Sie die Absage an Ihren alten Glauben hin und wieder bereut?

Professor Dr. Gerd Lüdemann: Nein, allerdings habe ich mich zwischenzeitlich gefragt, ob es klug war, diesen Schritt öffentlich zu machen, weil er zu erheblichen finanziellen Einbußen für meine Mitarbeiter geführt hat. Ich habe Drittmittelanträge nicht mehr durchbekommen, und auch andere Finanzquellen sind mittlerweile versiegt.

Kommentare: Wenn Sie Ihren Schritt nicht öffentlich gemacht hätten, hätten Sie sich viel Ärger erspart.

Lüdemann: Ja, aber ich wollte nicht mit den anderen schweigenden Fakultätskollegen die Frage nach der Wahrheit einfach aufgeben, nur um meinen Status quo zu erhalten.

Kommentare: Gehen Sie davon aus, daß andere Ihrer Kollegen in der gleichen Gewissensnot sind wie Sie, darüber aber nicht öffentlich reden?

Lüdemann: Ja.

Kommentare: Ihre wissenschaftliche Arbeit hat Sie in einen Konflikt mit der verfaßten Kirche geführt. Sind auch die damit verbundenen Erlebnisse ausschlaggebend für Ihren Abschied vom christlichen Glauben?

Lüdemann: Wenn mein Bischof, der hannoversche Landesbischof Horst Hirschler, behauptet, ich legte es darauf an, sanktioniert zu werden und er anschließend die öffentliche Diskussion ablehnt, hinterläßt das schon Spuren. Erfahrungen wie diese haben mich in dem Eindruck bestärkt, daß in der Kirche nicht mehr die Suche nach der Wahrheit im Vordergrund steht. Es scheint eine weitverbreitete stillschweigende Übereinkunft zu geben, die bestehenden Verhältnisse nicht grundsätzlich infragezustellen.

Kommentare: Sie reden von Wahrheit, und scheinen dabei ein sehr rationalistisches Verständnis zu haben. Müssen Sie nicht zugestehen, daß dies nur einem Teil der Wirklichkeit gerecht wird?

Lüdemann: Ich weiß, daß es verschiedene Ebenen von Wirklichkeit gibt. Das gestehe ich sofort zu. Mit Blick auf die biblischen Quellen geht es aber zunächst einmal darum festzustellen, welche Aussagen in ihnen wirklich gemacht werden.

Kommentare: Sie meinen, es geht um die Frage, ob das Grab voll oder leer war?

Lüdemann: Ja, das ist der Kernpunkt. Wenn die biblischen Quellen von der Auferstehung Jesu berichten, setzen sie einen wiederbelebten Leichnam voraus. Hier wird Wahrheit nicht symbolisch verstanden, sondern körperlich und historisch. Deswegen ist mein ursprünglicher Versuch, das leere Grab symbolisch zu interpretieren, gescheitert. Wer die Auferstehung Jesu nicht körperlich und historisch versteht, kann sich nicht auf die biblischen Quellen berufen.

Kommentare: Sie sehen einen Widerspruch zwischen wissenschaftlicher Theologie und kirchlicher Verkündigung. Wäre es da nicht konsequent, wenn Sie sich auch offiziell von der Kirche trennten?

Lüdemann: Es gibt zwei Gründe, warum ich nicht aus der Kirche austrete. Der erste ist beruflicher Natur. Ich spreche hier fast wie ein Gewerkschafter, denn mein Kirchenaustritt würde nach geltendem Recht dazu führen, daß ich meinen Lehrstuhl verliere. Das aber möchte ich vermeiden. Zum zweiten aber erhalte ich eine große Unterstützung von vielen Pfarrern. Mein Kirchenaustritt würde auf sie wie ein Schlag ins Gesicht wirken.

Kommentare: Welche Gründe haben die Pfarrer, Sie zu unterstützen?

Lüdemann: Darüber kann ich nur spekulieren. Aber wie zum Beispiel die jüngste Studie von Klaus-Peter Jörns zeigt, glauben auch die Pfarrer längst nicht mehr alles, worauf sie ordiniert worden sind. Sie haben aber keine Möglichkeit, ihre Zweifel vor der Gemeinde zu zeigen. Vielleicht stelle ich stellvertretend für sie ihre Fragen an die Kirche.

Kommentare: Sie beobachten demnach eine große Unaufrichtigkeit zwischen dem, was viele in der Kirche glauben und dem, was die offizielle Kirche nach außen darstellt?

Lüdemann: Ja, als ich noch in den kirchlichen Prüfungskommissionen vertreten war, habe ich oft erlebt, daß man mit Oberlandeskirchenräten beim Wein oder beim Kaffee locker über die menschliche Seite des frühen Christentums sprechen konnte. Dabei spielten dogmatische Dinge fast überhaupt keine Rolle. Problematisch wird es anscheinend erst dann, wenn man als öffentliche Person Stellung bezieht. Ich weigere mich aber mittlerweile, zwischen meinen Aussagen in der Öffentlichkeit und im privaten Bereich zu unterscheiden. Ich halte mich nicht mehr an die Spielregeln, die in der Kirche häufig gelten und werde deswegen mit Sanktionen belegt.

Kommentare: Trotzdem müssen Sie doch zugestehen, daß Ihre Weigerung, aus der Kirche auszutreten, inkonsequent ist.

Lüdemann: Ja, das sage ich auch ganz offen: Mein Verbleib in der Kirche ist eine Frage der Taktik. Damit unterscheide ich mich aber keineswegs vom Verhalten anderer Kollegen an unserer Fakultät.

Kommentare: Wie meinen Sie das?

Lüdemann: Mit als eine Konsequenz aus dem Streit um meine Person hat die Fakultät die sogenannte Gieselersche Formel aus dem Jahr 1848 wieder bekräftigt. Darin wird die Verpflichtung ausgesprochen, die theologischen Wissenschaften in Übereinstimmung mit den Grundsätzen der evangelisch-lutherischen Kirche vorzutragen. Ich frage mich, wie Kollegen die Gieselersche Formel sprechen können und gleichzeitig eine symbolische Interpretation der Auferstehung vertreten, wenn die

Bekenntnisse doch von einer körperlichen Auferstehung ausgehen. Dieses Vorgehen kann man auch als Taktik bezeichnen. Angesichts der Geltung der Bekenntnisse kommt eigentlich keiner in der Kirche ohne Taktik aus.

Kommentare: Auch der Bischof nicht?

Lüdemann: Auch Bischof Hirschler hat mir gegenüber einmal eingeräumt, daß seiner Meinung nach das Grab voll war und das auch als junger Pastor gepredigt hat. Wenn er nur einmal heute den Mut hätte, das auch in der Öffentlichkeit zu sagen! In einem Brief an mich bezeichnet er sich als Bultmann-Schüler. Auch Bultmann sagte, daß das Grab voll war.

Kommentare: Vermutlich ist Bischof Hirschler aber der Auffassung, daß es auf diese Frage eigentlich nicht ankommt, weil das Bekenntnis der geistlichen Erfahrung der ersten Christen Ausdruck gibt, aber keinen Anspruch auf Historizität erhebt.

Lüdemann: Das letztere bestreite ich entschieden. In jedem Fall ist es doppelbödig, wenn man die Fakten zugunsten ihrer Deutung auflöst.

Kommentare: Die dogmatischen Grundlagen der Kirche beruhen nun einmal auf einer bestimmten Deutung der geschichtlichen Überlieferung. Wenn Sie diese Deutung infrage stellen, stellen Sie die Grundlagen der Kirche infrage. Müssen Sie deshalb nicht damit rechnen, daß die Kirche empört reagiert?

Lüdemann: Das verstehe ich schon, aber ich finde es bedauerlich, daß sich die Kirche nur auf bestimmte Traditionen beruft, andere aber vernachlässigt; zum Beispiel den liberalen Protestantismus, oder auch andere Formen des Christentums, wie etwa die Quäker, die keine Bekenntnisse kennen. Die Kirche könnte sich ja ändern. Aber ich sehe in ihr viele, die ein Interesse daran haben, daß die Kirche bleibt, wie sie ist, weil auf diese Weise viele Vorteile – auch gesamtgesellschaftlicher Art – gewahrt werden. Dafür werden selbst Bibelverse instrumentalisiert.

Kommentare: Zum Beispiel?

Lüdemann: Zum Beispiel bei den Denkschriften oder dem Sozialwort der evangelischen und katholischen Kirche. Bei diesen Dokumenten habe ich den Eindruck, daß sie von gewieften Gesellschaftswissenschaftlern geschrieben und nachträglich biblisch begründet werden. Auf diese Weise wird die Bibel zu einem Steinbruch. Ich glaube, so kann die Kirche nicht weitermachen. Einerseits vertritt sie die alten Bekenntnisse, andererseits will sie völlig modern in einem säkularen Staat mitarbeiten. Das kann nicht funktionieren.

Kommentare: In früheren Zeiten hätte man jemanden wie Sie als Häretiker bezeichnet. Läßt sich der Begriff heute noch verwenden?

Lüdemann: Ich glaube nicht. Der Begriff Häretiker oder Ketzer hat heute eigentlich keine Bedeutung mehr. In einer freien Christengemeinde jedenfalls darf man den Begriff nicht gebrauchen. Denn hier sollte jede Meinung akzeptiert werden, soweit sie den anderen nicht bedroht oder beleidigt.

Kommentare: Aber es gibt in der Kirche doch eine verbindliche Lehre von der man abweichen und insofern auch zum Häretiker werden kann.

Lüdemann: Ich finde, die gibt es nicht. Und es muß sie meines Erachtens auch nicht geben. Denn die Lehre ist eine Reflexion des gelebten Glaubens. Die Kirche lebt aber nicht aus der Rechtgläubigkeit, sondern aus Singen, Beten und dem Feiern des Gottesdienstes. Religion kann auch ohne Theologie leben, die Theologie aber nicht ohne Religion. Das ist die Reihenfolge.

Kommentare: Ihre anfechtbaren Auffassungen wirken sich vermutlich stark auf das Klima innerhalb der theologischen Fakultät in Göttingen aus. Wie verhalten sich Ihre Kollegen Ihnen gegenüber?

Lüdemann: Das Kollegium hat kürzlich mit fünfzehn Stimmen zu einer dem Präsidenten der Universität empfohlen, mich aus der theologischen Fakultät auszugliedern. Es gab vorher eine Stellungnahme am 22. April 1998, daß die Kollegen, im Unterschied zu mir, den christlichen Glauben und die Wissenschaft von vornherein für vereinbar halten. Hinter den Kulissen sieht es aber etwas anders aus. Da sichert mir der eine oder andere durchaus Solidarität zu. Aber der Druck, den die hannoversche Landeskirche auf die Fakultät ausübt, ist enorm. Ohne diesen Druck wäre das Votum der Kollegen gegen mich wahrscheinlich nicht zustande gekommen.

Kommentare: Kritik erfahren Sie nicht nur aus dem Bereich der Kirche, sondern auch aus der Theologie. Bedenken gibt es vor allem gegen Ihre wissenschaftlichen Methoden. Sie arbeiteten mit Mitteln des vorigen Jahrhunderts, lautet der Vorwurf.

Lüdemann: Ich stehe in der Tradition Rudolf Bultmanns und verwende die Methoden der Religionsgeschichtlichen Schule, deren Archiv ich gegründet habe und leite. Insofern könnte man sagen, daß ich eine konservative Methodik vertrete, weil ich die neueren Wendungen zum Strukturalismus oder zur Linguistik nicht mitgemacht habe. Das heißt aber nicht, daß ich ein Außenseiter in der Forschung wäre. Meiner Beobachtung nach teilen die meisten Bibelforscher meinen methodischen Ansatz.

Kommentare: In dem Interview, das wir vor dreieinhalb Jahren mit Ihnen geführt haben und das der eigentliche Ausgangspunkt für die Kontroverse um Ihre Person wurde, haben Sie den ordinierten Theologen Heuchelei vorgeworfen. Bleiben Sie dabei, oder hat sich der Vorwurf als zu pauschal herausgestellt?

Lüdemann: Ich habe nicht die Pastoren kritisiert, sondern die Kirche, und zwar insofern, als die Pastoren auf etwas ordiniert werden, was sie nicht glauben können. Das wird ja auch durch die jüngste Untersuchung von Klaus-Peter Jörns bestätigt. Ich bin weiter davon überzeugt, daß mein Vorwurf der Scheinheiligkeit gerechtfertigt ist.

Kommentare: Heißt das, die Kirche hat Sie falsch interpretiert?

Lüdemann: Sie hat meine Bemerkungen als Verleumdung ihres ordinierenden Handelns interpretiert und als Angriff auf die Pastoren. Dabei will ich doch nur die Pastoren gegenüber der Kirche in Schutz nehmen.

Kommentare: Müßten Sie dann nicht sogar die Theologiestudierenden davor warnen, sich für ein kirchliches Amt ausbilden zu lassen?

Lüdemann: Das ist schon wahr, denn im Grunde stellt das Vorgehen der wissenschaftlichen Theologen die Spitze der Heuchelei dar. Indem sie den Studierenden die Ergebnisse der historisch-kritischen Forschung vermitteln, nehmen sie ihnen den Glauben der Bekenntnisse, den sie in ihrem kirchlichen Dienst vertreten sollen. Das ist das Fatale.

Kommentare: Ihr Status an der theologischen Fakultät ist umstritten. Wie sehen Sie ihren weiteren beruflichen Weg?

Lüdemann: In einem Brief vom 17. Dezember 1998 hat mir der Präsident der Universität Göttingen mitgeteilt, daß ich mit einem Sonderstatus in der theologischen Fakultät bleibe, und zwar als Professor für "Geschichte und Literatur des frühen Christentums". Ich betrachte diese Lösung als Teilsieg meinerseits und als eine Bestätigung dafür, daß auch ein Nicht-

Christ Theologieprofessor sein kann. Das nämlich ist die Voraussetzung dafür, daß es eines Tages theologische Fakultäten gibt, die nicht mehr nach Konfessionen organisiert sind.

Kommentare: Der Entscheidung des Präsidenten ist das Wissenschaftsministerium aber nur teilweise gefolgt. Minister Oppermann hat jüngst deren vorläufigen Charakter betont. Weitere Rechtsfragen sollen auf Wunsch der Konföderation der Evangelischen Kirchen in Niedersachsen weiter geprüft werden. Außerdem dürfen Sie auch keine Religionslehrer mehr ausbilden. Wie beurteilen Sie diese Zuspitzung?

Lüdemann: Zunächst bin ich erleichtert, daß ich vorerst überhaupt an der theologischen Fakultät verbleibe. Gleichzeitig aber bin ich erschrocken, wie brutal die Konföderation vorgegangen ist. Ich bin nun nämlich jeglicher Beteiligung an der akademischen Ausbildung beraubt.

Kommentare: Sie dürfen also in keinem Studiengang mehr Scheine ausstellen und Prüfungen abnehmen?

Lüdemann: Ja, weder innerhalb der staatlichen theologischen Diplomprüfung noch im Rahmen der Gymnasiallehrerausbildung im Fach "Evangelische Religion". Das Fach soll an der Schule offenbar wieder Katechismusunterricht werden. Mein einziges Vergehen, für das ich abgestraft werde, ist ein historisches Ergebnis, das im Widerspruch zu den Grundsätzen der evangelischen Kirche steht. Die evangelische Kirche vertritt im Streit gegen mich eine erzkatholische Position.

Kommentare: Inwiefern?

Lüdemann: Sie entspricht dem sogenannten Antimodernisteneid aus dem Jahre 1910. Danach mußte jeder Professor und Priester schwören: "Ich verwerfe den Irrtum jener, die behaupten, daß der von der Kirche vorgetragene Glaube der Geschichte widerstreiten kann." Ein solcher Eid aber kann nicht im Sinne der evangelischen Kirche sein.

Mit Professor Dr. Gerd Lüdemann sprachen Michael Strauß und Götz Planer-Friedrich am 28. Januar und 9. Februar in Göttingen.

20

Statement (10.02.1999) of the Dean in Regard to the Academic Position to be Held by Professor Dr. Gerd Lüdemann

Prof. Dr. Eberhard Busch, Dean.

On December 17, 1998, the President of the Georgia Augusta University of Göttingen, Prof.Dr. Horst Kern, made known the following decision which was confirmed on February 4, 1999, by the Minister for Arts and Sciences in Lower Saxony, Thomas Oppermann, after due consultation with the said President, the Dean of the Theological Faculty, and the representatives of the Confederation of Evangelical Churches in Lower Saxony, all of whom gave their consent:

Effective immediately, Prof. Dr. Gerd Lüdemann is being assigned the field of "History and Literature of Early Christianity" for his teaching and research. While Prof. Lüdemann remains affiliated with the Theological Faculty, his status is affected as follows:

1. The reassignment of Prof. Lüdemann's position in New Testament Studies entails a detachment from the "Vereinigte Theologische Seminare" (United Theology Departments) and relocation in the Institute for Special Studies and Research.
2. Courses taught by Prof. Lüdemann are to be explicitly identified as "outside of the programs of study required for the training of future ministers of the Church, including the field of Christian Education."

The Dean of the Theological Faculty releases the following statement:

a. This decision was made necessary not because of specific critical statements or claims of research by Prof. Lüdemann but because he has denied the scholarly validity of Protestant theology and thus no longer sees his mission as the preparation of students seeking to become ministers of the Church.

b. Prof. Lüdemann did not see fit to take the obvious step of resigning from his position in the Protestant Theological Faculty, whose purpose he no longer acknowledges or supports. His colleagues, the professors belonging to our Faculty, have asserted repeatedly – the last such meeting having taken place on December 12, 1998 – that with his statements and claims made in public, Prof. Lüdemann has in fact placed himself outside of our Faculty.

c. The Ministry for Arts and Sciences (Ministerium) in Hannover has demonstrated its concurrence in that, as early as the summer of 1998, it authorized a replacement in the form of a new Chair of New Testament Studies. This was done in accordance with the church-state agreement (Loccumer Vertrag) to provide the instruction necessary for the academic training of students of theology, which is no longer being offered by Prof. Lüdemann.

d. This decision as it stands, determined by the President of the University of Göttingen and confirmed by the Minister for Arts and Sciences in Hannover, was reached only after it had become clear that the Philosophical Faculty at the University of Göttingen was unwilling to admit Prof. Lüdemann to their membership, and that all other possibilities were either of doubtful legal validity or otherwiseimpracticable.

e. While a decision of this kind does not fall within the jurisdiction of the Theological Faculty, the President of the University asked for and received the advice of the professors before stating his decision; the faculty committee let it be known, as of December 14, 1998, that, as matters stand, the Faculty is ready to concur with the President's decision.

f. At no time has the Faculty sought to restrict the liberties of Prof. Lüdemann. To the contrary, it has concerned itself with the difficult problem, in the resolution of which Prof. Lüdemann has not been cooperative – i.e., the question: In the University system, what kind of place and position can be made available for a professor, who, according to German law, has the irrevocable status of a civil servant, but who at the same time rejects the basic principles of the institution to which he belongs and which he, at the time of his installation as professor, committed himself to serve?

g.   According to the minutes of the Faculty committee meeting of December 14, 1998, this decision represents no more than a make-shift solution ("Notlösung"). This make-shift solution places a heavy burden on all concerned. The Theological Faculty has accepted this decision only because of the stipulation that the academic activities of Prof. Lüdemann are relegated to an area "outside of the programs of study required for the training of future ministers of the Church." The details of this arrangement have yet to be determined.

h.   It is clear from all that has been said that the decision in the case of Prof. Lüdemann does not constitute a precedent in regard to the status of the Protestant Theological Faculty. That no change in status is intended is also made clear by the fact that this make-shift solution will cease with the departure of Prof. Lüdemann as professor at the University of Göttingen.

i.   It is my hope that this make-shift solution will help to restore the atmosphere conducive to research and studies to which our Faculty and students are accustomed, but which has, in recent months, been disrupted by this affair. We are especially grateful that the field of New Testament will be maintained in its former size through the granting of two full professorships.

ERKLÄRUNG DES DEKANS VOM **10.02.1999** ZUR ENTSCHEIDUNG HINSICHTLICH DER KÜNFTIGEN AKADEMISCHEN STELLUNG VON PROF. DR. GERD LÜDEMANN

Am 17.12.1998 hat der Präsident der Georg-August-Universität Göttingen, Prof. Dr. Horst Kern, in dieser Angelegenheit eine Entscheidung getroffen, die am 4.2.1999 von dem niedersächsischen Minister für Wissenschaft und Kunst, Thomas Oppermann, nach Anhörung des Präsidenten, des Dekans und der Vertreter der nieders. Konföderation der evangelischen Kirchen und unter deren Zustimmung bis aus weiteres in Kraft gesetzt wurde. Demnach wird mit sofortiger Wirkung Prof. Dr. Gerd Lüdemann zur Vertretung des Fachs "Geschichte und Literatur des Frühen Christentums" verpflichtet. Zwar bleibt Herr Lüdemann der Theologischen Fakultät zugeordnet, jedoch hat dies für seinen Status weitreichende Konsequenzen:

1.   Die Umwidmung seines bisher vertretenen Faches Neues Testament ist verbunden mit der Ausgliederung aus den "Vereinigten Theologischen Seminaren" und der Zuweisung zum "Institut für Spezialforschungen".

2. Seine Tätigkeit ist künftig ausdrücklich zu kennzeichnen mit dem Zusatz "außerhalb der Studiengänge zur Ausbildung des theologischen Nachwuchses (einschließlich des Faches Religionspädagogik)".

Der Dekan der Theologischen Fakultät erklärt zu der getroffenen Entscheidung folgendes:

a. Eine Entscheidung war nötig geworden nicht wegen einzelner kritischer Äußerungen von Herrn Lüdemann, sondern weil er der evangelischen Theologie die Wissenschaftlichkeit abgesprochen und darum auch seine Aufgabe nicht mehr in der Ausbildung des theologischen Nachwuchses gesehen hat.

b. Herr Lüdemann war nicht bereit, für sich die naheliegende Konsequenz zu ziehen, die Evangelisch-theologische Fakultät zu verlassen, obwohl er deren Sinn und Aufgabe nicht mehr anerkennt und vertritt. Daraufhin haben die Professoren unserer Fakultät ihrerseits mehrfach, zuletzt am 12.12.1998 festgestellt, daß Herr Lüdemann mit seinen öffentlichen Erklärungen den Raum der Fakultät faktisch verlassen hat.

c. Das Ministerium in Hannover hat sich diese Feststellung im Kern zu eigen gemacht, indem es schon im Sommer 1998 einen Ersatz geschaffen und einen Lehrstuhl für Neues Testament eingerichtet hat. Der Zweck dieser Maßnahme ist, daß auf diesem Lehrstuhl die staatskirchenrechtlich geregelten Aufgaben wahrgenommen werden, die Herr Lüdemann nicht mehr erfüllt.

d. Der Göttinger Universitätspräsident hat seine genannte Entscheidung gefällt und der Minister hat sie bestätigt, nachdem sich die Philosophische Fakultät nicht bereitgefunden hatte, Herrn Lüdemann aufzunehmen, und andere Lösungen rechtlich bedenklich und praktisch schwer durchführbar erschienen.

e. Die theologische Fakultät ist in dieser Sache kein Entscheidungsgremium. Der Präsident hat sich aber vor seiner Entscheidung durch das Professorium beraten lassen, und der Fakultätsrat hat am 14.12.1998 signalisiert, daß er unter den gegebenen Umständen die Entscheidung des Präsidenten anzuerkennen bereit ist.

f. Die Fakultät hatte zu keinem Zeitpunkt die Absicht, die Freiheitsrechte von Herrn Lüdemann zu beschneiden. Es ging ihr vielmehr um die schwierige Frage, zu deren Lösung Herr Lüdemann nicht von sich aus behilflich war: Wie läßt sich für einen nicht absetzbaren professoralen Beamten, der die Grundlagen der Institution, der er angehört und verpflichtet ist, bestreitet, ein Platz an der Universität ausmachen?

g. Die Entscheidung stellt in dieser schwierigen Situation eine "Notlösung" dar, wie der Fakultätsrat am 14.12.1998 festgestellt hat. Diese Notlösung ist allen Beteiligten beschwerlich. Diese Notlösung kann von der Theologischen Fakultät nur deshalb akzeptiert werden, weil damit Herrn Lüdemanns Tätigkeit auf einen Bereich "außerhalb der Studiengänge zur Ausbildung des theologischen Nachwuchses" eingegrenzt ist. Die Konsequenzen, die sich daraus ergeben, sind in den Einzelheiten noch zu fixieren.

h. Nach dem allen ist die Entscheidung nicht als Präzedenzfall anzusehen, der den Status der Evangelisch-theologischen Fakultät verändert. Das wird auch dadurch unterstrichen, daß die gefundene Notlösung spätestens zu dem Zeitpunkt erlöschen wird, an dem Herr Lüdemann aus seiner Professur ausscheidet.

i. Ich hoffe, daß die Notlösung dazu beiträgt, daß nach den allzu spektakulären Vorgängen der letzten Monate in dieser Angelegenheit unsere Fakultät sich nunmehr wieder ungestört auf ihre wissenschaftliche Aufgabe konzentrieren kann. Wir sind dankbar, daß dabei namentlich die Wahrnehmung der theologischen Lehre im Neuen Testament durch zwei volle C 4-Stellen sichergestellt ist.

Professor Dr. E. Busch
Dekan

21

Letters of Concern for Prof. Dr. Gerd Lüdemann

Fellows of the Jesus Seminar

March 21, 2000

Minister Thomas Oppermann
Minister fuer Wissenschaft und Kultur
Leibnizufer 9
30169 Hannover
Germany

Prof. Dr. Horst Kern
Praesident der Georg-August-Universitaet
Gosslerstr. 5/7
37073 Goettingen
Germany

Prof. Dr. Anneli Aejmelaeus
Dekanin der Evangelisch-Theologischen Fakultaet
Platz der Goettinger Sieben 2
37073 Goettingen
Germany

Cc: Chancellor Gerhard Schroeder

Dear Mr. Oppermann, Prof. Kern, and Prof. Aejmelaeus:

We are writing to you out of concern for the situation of our colleague, Prof. Dr. Gerd Lüdemann. We have followed his situation with keen interest because it involves the freedom of professors to express freely the ideas that will ultimately lead to progress and clarity in the field of theology. We understand that the manner of pursuing theological education is different in Germany from the way things are done here in the United States. We also understand that the relationship of the church to theological faculties in your state universities is quite foreign to our way of thinking about state-sponsored education. However, taking all of this into account, we still find reason to be distressed over Prof. Lüdemann's situation.

To many of us it seems right and appropriate that the church should show proper concern for the education of its clergy, and to exercise some control over who should participate in the process of qualifying students for ordination. Thus, it does not trouble us that Prof. Lüdemann may no longer read the church exams, or offer courses to students preparing for ordination to the ministry, even though many of us believe that Prof. Lüdemann's ideas might even prove helpful to the church as it seeks to clarify the meaning of Christian faith in the Twenty-First Century. That the Theological Faculty has not seen the opportunity to engage Prof. Lüdemann's ideas within the context of its theological work is quite unfortunate, and represents a loss to the quality of the intellectual environment.

What is most distressing to us is the fact that Prof. Lüdemann has also been barred from reading the faculty exams, advising doctoral students, and evaluating the work of Dozents. None of these educational programs necessarily involves the training of persons to serve in the church. That the state, through the offices of the University and the Theological Faculty, should bar him from participating fully in these areas is a grave stroke against academic freedom. The issue here is not the quality or persuasiveness of Prof. Lüdemann's views. In fact, many of us have criticized his ideas, even as he has criticized ours. The issue is the free exchange of ideas, in print, and in the classroom. It is our understanding that through the actions taken by the University and the Theological Faculty, Prof. Lüdemann has effectively been barred from offering courses or advising students. This goes to the heart of academic freedom. The classroom is above all the place where academic freedom must be exercised. Without this, there is no real academic freedom. And without academic freedom, there is no intellectual integrity.

We understand that our ways are different here in the United States, and that the University must balance the interests of both the church and the broader culture in this matter. We realize that this is not an easy thing to do. And we appreciate the fact that thus far the University, the Theological Faculty, and the Ministry of Science and Culture have sought a solution that does not involve the dismissal of Prof. Lüdemann altogether, as the church had apparently desired. Still, the present situation has left Prof. Lüdemann without a voice in the classroom. We would therefore urge you all to seek a new solution to the problem, one that restores to Prof. Lüdemann an active role in the education of students who are not necessarily preparing for ordination in the Lutheran church. This would include offering courses with credit to students who are not preparing for ordained ministry, participating in the Faculty Exams, advising doctoral students, and evaluating the work of Dozents.

As we enter a new millennium, it has become clear that one of the tasks that lies before us in the west is a critical coming to grips with our Christian past. This is a task not only for the church, but for everyone who is an heir to this cultural legacy. This is precisely what Prof. Lüdemann is asking us to do, albeit in a very provocative way. That this challenge should be taken out of the theological curriculum altogether is a travesty. Is there a more important issue with which our students should be forced to struggle at this critical time in our history? We do not think so. That is why we are asking you to reconsider this situation, and to find a new solution that reaffirms his right to engage in full academic discussion of his research regardless of its results or his personal views.

Sincerely Yours,

Robert W. Funk

Director, Westar Institute
Chair, Jesus Seminar
on behalf of the Fellows of the Jesus Seminar

Signatories

Robert W. Funk, Ph.D. [Westar Institute]
Valerie Abrahamsen, Th.D., [Jamaica Plain]
Robert W. Allison, [Bates College]
Ed Beutner, Ph.D. [Our Lady Queen of the Universe, Woodruff, WI]
Marvin F. Cain, Ph.D. [Lutheran pastor. Mid-Columbia Center for Theological Studies]
Kathleen E. Corley. Ph.D. [University of Wisconsin-Oshkosh]
Jon B. Daniels, Ph.D. [Arizona State University]
Arthur J. Dewey, Th.D. [Xavier University]
Darrell Doughty, D.Theol. [Drew University]
Susan M. Elliott Ph.D. [Sterling, Colorado]
Lloyd Geering, D.D., [Victoria University, Wellington, New Zealand]
Stephen L. Harris, Ph.D., [California State University, Sacramento]
Roy W. Hoover, Ph.D. [emeritus, Whitman College]
Glenna S. Jackson, Ph.D. [Otterbein College]
Gregory C. Jenks, Ph.D. [Westar Institute]
Karen King, Ph.D. [Harvard Divinity School]
Davidson Loehr, Ph.D. [Unity Church, St. Paul, MN]
Perry V. Kea, Ph.D. [University of Indianapolis]

Brian R. McCarthy, S.T.M. [Madison, WI]
Lane McGaughy, Ph.D. [Willamette University]
Robert J. Miller, Ph.D. [Midway College]
Culver H. Nelson, L.H.D., D.D [Holmes Institute]
Steven J. Patterson, Ph.D. [Eden Theological Seminary]
Robert M. Price, Ph.D. [Center for Inquiry Institute]
Daryl D. Schmidt, Ph.D. [Texas Christian University]
Chris Shea, Ph.D. [Ball State University]
Thomas Sheehan, Ph.D. [Stanford University]
Dennis E. Smith, Ph.D. [Phillips Theological Seminary]
Mahlon Smith, M.S.L. (Pontifical Institute) [Rutgers University]
Graydon F. Snyder, Th.D. [Chicago Theological Seminary]
Johan Strijdom, [University of South Africa, South Africa]
W. Barnes Tatum. Ph.D. [Greensboro College]
Hal Taussig, Ph.D. [Union Theological Seminary]
Barbara Thiering, Ph.D. [University of Sydney, Australia]
Joseph B. Tyson, Ph.D. [emeritus, Southern Methodist University]
James A. Veitch, Ph.D. [Victoria University, Wellington, New Zealand]
Theodore J. Weeden, Ph.D. [emeritus, Colgate Rochester Divinity School]
Sara Winter, Ph.D. [New School for Social Research]

Second Letter on Behalf of Prof. Dr. Gerd Lüdemann

by Robert W. Funk

June 30, 2000

Prof. Dr. E. Muehlenberg
Faculty of Theology
George-August University
37073 Goettingen
Germany

Dear Prof. Dr. Muehlenberg:

I write in response to your letter of April 4, 2000.

Although an "open letter" would have been quite appropriate in such a case, it was not our intention that you would learn about our letter from in the press. As indicated in the covering note that accompanied the original text of our letter, the early publication in Die Welt was an unfortunate turn of events and we regret any embarrassment that it may have caused. While we will, in the future, attempt to address you more directly, it is not our intention to do so privately.

This is, in our view, not a private matter to be worked out among colleagues.

It is a public matter, which concerns anyone who cares about religious and academic freedom. It is not a private relationship that compels us to address you, but our common responsibility to speak openly and honestly about matters that affect the public discussion of religion in our common culture.

The ocean that divides is not so deep as you might think. The names David Friedrich Strauss, Albert Schweitzer, and Rudolf Bultmann are just as familiar here as they are among you. American protestant theology has for years relied on the tradition of critical German scholarship to press us beyond the comfortable limits of conventional thinking, to explore new frontiers in theology. That is why the case of Gerd Lüdemann is of interest to us. Regardless of whether we agree with his views, that he should be sanctioned for his (admittedly provocative) challenge to conventional theological wisdom, is a thing of grave concern for us.

Your letter makes a number of assertions to which we must respond.

First, you have charged that we have acted without knowing all sides of the story. This may be so, although we have availed ourselves of the public documents pertaining to the case. If our letter indicates that we have misunderstood the limits that have been placed upon Prof. Lüdemann's teaching, we would expect you to set the record straight for us. Moreover, if we have misunderstood the role played by the faculty in bringing about the decision to alter his status, we would welcome your clarification of the matter. We do have the text of the resolution of the faculty passed on 18 November 1998, asking that Prof. Lüdemann be removed from the Theological Faculty.

Second, you have criticized us for not recognizing that the decision to alter Prof. Lüdemann's status was taken not by the church or by the theological faculty, but by the university and the Ministry of Culture. We are, of course, aware of the official process by which Prof. Lüdemann's fate was decided. But this in no way relieves the theological faculty of its responsibility and role in the matter. Was it not the resolution of the faculty that placed Prof. Lüdemann's status in question in the first place? What role the church might have played in this process is unclear to us. Nonetheless, that you should minimize the impact of your own actions, while appealing to the decision of higher authorities, is most unsettling.

So, too, is your appeal to the authority of the German courts. We are, of course, aware that the courts have refused to grant Lüdemann an injunction against the decision of the university. But this does not resolve the matter. The case is still before the German courts, and will be subject to appeal. In any event, this is a very complicated case that will likely involve considering certain provisions of your Grundgesetz regarding the relationship between church and state. You will need to be part of that discussion. The church will need to be part of that discussion. You cannot abdicate your responsibility to participate in this decision by appealing to state authorities.

Having clarified these matters, we must now insist that you have not responded to our most fundamental point: that Prof. Lüdemann ought to be allowed to teach students who are not preparing for ordination in the Lutheran Church. This is based on the conviction that a public university ought to serve all the legitimate interests of the pluralistic society which supports it.

We realize that the status of theological faculties in German universities rests on a complex history, which we may not fully understand from our point of view here in the United States. And we recognize the need of the church to impose limits on what is to be considered doctrinally acceptable, and what is not.

We understand that this is a lesson you have learned in a most difficult way during the period of the Third Reich. Still, do you really believe that a theological faculty should not include voices that, in view of their own research, are very critical of church doctrine? Many of our private, church-supported seminaries now include professors who are Jewish, some even, who teach in the area of New Testament. And their presence has not harmed the church in any way. To the contrary, it has enriched the environment for preparing church leaders to serve the church in a pluralistic culture. How much more would this be true in your own publicly-supported institutions? And even if someone like Prof. Lüdemann could not legitimately participate in those areas of the curriculum devoted to the preparation of candidates for ordained ministry, why should he not participate in those areas that are not devoted expressly to this function?

Here is the issue as we see it: Do the theological faculties of your state universities serve only the church, or do they also serve the broader needs of a pluralistic culture? If the latter is true, then voices critical of the church, its history, or its doctrines, ought not be excluded entirely from the lecture halls of the Theological Faculty. A pluralistic culture thrives on free

thought. This much is basic. Some would even argue that the church can only be authentic when it, too, welcomes free and critical thought. Was this not the conviction of Luther, Schleiermacher, Troeltsch, Tillich, and so many others who have made the German theological tradition such an important part of western culture?

With such a tradition upon which to rest, what does the Theological Faculty of Goettingen have to fear from Gerd Lüdemann?

Sincerely yours,

Robert W. Funk
Director, Westar Institute
Chair, Jesus Seminar on behalf of the Fellows of the Jesus Seminar

Copies to: Chancellor Gerhard Schroeder
Minister Thomas Oppermann
Prof. Dr. Horst Kern
Prof. Dr. Gerd Lüdemann

22

Im Würgegriff der Kirche

Muß ein Theologe Christ sein? Der Fall Lüdemann - Ein Exempel

Christoph Türcke

DIE ZEIT Nr. 41 vom 1. Oktober 1998

Gerd Lüdemann soll die Theologische Fakultät Göttingen verlassen, weil er nicht mehr an Sühnetod und göttliche Herkunft Jesu glaubt.

"Eine Wissenschaft vom christlichen Glauben ist sowenig christlich wie die Wissenschaft vom Verbrechen verbrecherisch", schrieb der Theologe Oskar Pfister 1923. Würden sich die deutschen Theologischen Fakultäten dieser Einsicht öffnen, müßten sie schließen. Aber sie brauchen nicht, denn sie sind gesetzlich geschützt. Besondere Verträge mit dem Staat garantieren den christlichen Kirchen konfessionellen Religionsunterricht an staatlichen Schulen und konfessionelle Theologie an staatlichen Universitäten. Wer nicht katholisch oder evangelisch getauft ist und die entsprechende Kirchensteuer zahlt, darf Religionsunterricht nicht erteilen; wer Theologieprofessor werden will, braucht zudem ein positives Gutachten der zuständigen Diözese oder Landeskirche.

Und die Kirchen tun, als sei das das Selbstverständlichste von der Welt. War's nicht immer so? Verdankt sich die europäische Universität nicht gar dem Christentum? Wohl wahr. Als im 12. und 13. Jahrhundert die Universitäten von Bologna und Paris von sich reden machten, da wurde der fortgeschrittenste Stand des Wissens von Theologen vorgetragen, da war die theologische Fakultät die höchste. Allerdings war da auch die Zugehörigkeit zur Gesellschaft zugleich Zwangsmitgliedschaft in der allein seligmachenden Kirche und das Abweichen von ihrer Lehre ein Kapitalverbrechen.

Diese Zeiten sind vorbei. Das Christentum ist nicht mehr der kulturelle Leim einer ganzen Gesellschaft, sondern nur noch ein Ferment darin. Ein Menschenrecht namens Religionsfreiheit hat sich durchgesetzt. Vom 17. bis zum 19. Jahrhundert ist es von Freigeistern, Aufklärern, Bürger—und Arbeitervereinen mühsam erkämpft worden—gegen erbitterten kirchlichen Widerstand. Seit aber die kirchliche Macht nicht mehr ausreicht, es zu verhindern, gehören die Kirchen zu denen, die es am lautesten für sich reklamieren. Wir wollen nur das Recht, unsern Glauben praktizieren zu dürfen wie jede andere Religionsgemeinschaft auch, beteuern sie. Doch wenn sie "Recht" sagen, meinen sie "Vorrecht". Eintreibung der Kirchensteuer durch den Staat, christlicher Religionsunterricht als reguläres Schulfach, konfessionsgebundene Theologie im gleichen wissenschaftlichen Rang an der Universität wie Physik, Mathematik oder Soziologie: all das, was in unserm Kulturkreis sämtlichen andern Glaubensgemeinschaften im Namen der Religionsfreiheit verwehrt wird und was die Großkirchen nur dürfen, weil sie es früher durften, als sie für das Menschenrecht der Religionsfreiheit noch der größte Hemmschuh waren, das soll ihnen selbstverständlich bleiben.

Von Zeit zu Zeit regt sich öffentliche Empörung dagegen, wie in Deutschland zuletzt im Fall Küngs, jenes katholischen Theologen, der die Unfehlbarkeit des Papstes angezweifelt, ein abweichendes Verständnis von Christsein entfaltet hatte und nach vielem Hin und Her die kirchliche Lehrbefugnis entzogen bekam. Als halbwegs aufgeklärter Zeitgenosse schüttelte man damals den Kopf über die Engstirnigkeit der obersten Glaubensaufsichtsbehörde in Rom.. Daß Küng, als er die Tübinger Fakultät der Katholischen Theologie verlassen mußte, dem Rektor der Universität direkt unterstellt wurde, sein eigenes Institut und alle akademischen Ehren bekam, nahm man als gerechten Ausgleich und moralischen Sieg einer weltoffeneren Theologie.

Nun haben die evangelischen Kirchen, die sich damals am öffentlichen Kopfschütteln kräftig beteiligten, ihren eigenen Fall, und dessen Stachel geht tiefer. Gerd Lüdemann, 1983 als ordentlicher Professor für Neues Testament an die Evangelisch-Theologische Fakultät der Universität Göttingen mit voller kirchlicher Zustimmung berufen, ist im Laufe des letzten Jahrzehnts durch seine wissenschaftliche Arbeit, die sogenannte historisch-kritische Bibelforschung, zu unerwarteten Ergebnissen gekommen. Die zahllosen Unstimmigkeiten und Unredlichkeiten, die ihm in den biblischen Texten aufstießen, haben ihn nach und nach davon überzeugt, daß weder Jesus auferstanden noch die Bibel göttliches Wort sei. Daraus hat er die Konsequenz gezogen: Sein Buch "Der große Betrug" (zu Klampen Verlag, 1998), das aus der Spreu der vielen Jesus untergeschobenen Bibelworte die wenigen herausarbeitet, die er mit gewisser Wahrscheinlichkeit so oder ähnlich gesagt haben könnte, hat einen spektakulären Auftakt. Es beginnt mit einem Abschiedsbrief an den "Herrn Jesus": nimmt Abschied von allem, was das Christentum diesem Jesus nachträglich angehängt hat: seinem Sühnetod für unsere Sünden, seiner Gottessohnschaft, Auferstehung und rettenden Wiederkunft.

Damit war das Maß voll. War Lüdemann schon die kirchliche Prüfungserlaubnis entzogen worden, als er Jesu Auferstehung bestritt, so verlangten nun seine Göttinger Fakultätskollegen in einer gemeinsamen Erklärung seinen Austritt aus der Theologischen Fakultät. Ein Nichtchrist könne nicht weiterhin Theologieprofessor sein. Die Konföderation Evangelischer Kirchen in Niedersachsen griff diese Forderung auf und teilte Lüdemann Mitte Juli schriftlich mit, das kirchliche Gutachten für seine Berufung nach Göttingen müsse "mit allen Konsequenzen zurückgenommen werden. Diese Rücknahme muß nach unserer Auffassung dazu führen, daß Sie die Theologische Fakultät verlassen." Professor dürfe er gerne bleiben, aber nicht für Theologie. Man gab Lüdemann sechs Wochen Zeit zu einer Stellungnahme, aber schon nach zwei Wochen vermeldete der Evangelische Pressedienst (epd) eine "Einigung" zwischen dem Ministerium für Wissenschaft und Kultur und den Evangelischen Landeskirchen: An der Göttinger Fakultät solle für "Ersatz im Fach Neues Testament" gesorgt werden.

Lüdemann freilich denkt nicht daran, seinen Lehrstuhl zu räumen, und er tritt auch nicht aus der Kirche aus, weil die ihn dann nach geltender Rechtslage sofort aus der Fakultät entfernen könnte. "Ich will an der Theologischen Fakultät nur weiter tun dürfen, was ich bei meiner Habilitation versprochen habe: der Wissenschaft dienen und die akademische Jugend im Geist der Wahrheit erziehen", heißt es in seiner Stellungnahme vom August 1998 an die Konföderation, und sein neuestes Buch "Im Würgeggriff der Kirche" (zu Klampen Verlag, 1998) ist der ausführliche Kommentar dazu: ein Manifest "Für die Freiheit der theologischen Wissenschaft".

Es wurmt die Protestanten schon lange, daß ihr Vertrag mit dem Staat nicht so straff ausgefallen ist wie der katholische. Die Katholiken haben besser vorgesorgt: rechtsverbindlich festschreiben lassen, daß das kirchliche Gutachten für einen vom Glauben abfallenden Theologieprofessor jederzeit zurückgenommen werden kann, derjenige dann die Fakultät verlassen und das zuständige Ministerium Ersatz schaffen muß. Das hat der evangelische Staatsvertrag versäumt. "Eine nachträgliche Beanstandung kennt das Vertragsrecht für die evangelische Kirche nicht. Dementsprechend sind Abhilfe oder Ersatzgestellungspflichten für den Staat nicht vorgesehen", räumt der Leiter des Kirchenrechtlichen Instituts der Evangelischen Kirche in Deutschland, Axel von Campenhausen, in seinem Standardwerk Staatskirchenrecht ein und legt das so aus: "Aus der fehlenden Regelung in den Verträgen folgen weder der Ausschluß einer kirchlichen Beanstandung noch deren Unbeachtlichkeit. Die Lehrverantwortung ist auch für die evangelische Kirche unverzichtbar." Daher könne ihr "ein nachträgliches Beanstandungsrecht [...] von Seiten des Staates nicht versagt werden".

Das wird man sehen. Vorerst ist nur das kirchliche Gutachten für Lüdemann zurückgenommen. Der offizielle Antrag auf seine Entfernung aus der Theologischen Fakultät ist noch nicht formuliert. Erst wenn er vorliegt, heißt es im Ministerium, werde man prüfen, ob Lüdemann auch gegen seinen Willen in eine andere Fakultät umgesetzt werden könne. Aber schon vorher hat die Landesregierung bemerkenswerte Konzessionen gemacht: "Zwischen Universität, Ministerium und Kirchen wurde jetzt eine Regelung entwickelt, nach der freiwerdende andere Lehrstühle im Fachbereich Theologie jeweils auf Zeit mit einem Lehrbefähigten für das Fach Neues Testament besetzt werden." Zudem "könnte im Jahr 2002 eine C4-Professur aus einem anderen Fachbereich an die Theologie gehen", berichtet epd.

Die Kirche nimmt das als feste Zusage. Sie ist in der Offensive. Sie hat Fakten geschaffen. Sie hat Lüdemann die kirchliche Prüfungserlaubnis entzogen, sie erkennt bei ihm gemachte Seminarscheine nicht mehr an. Also ist ein ordnungsgemäßes Studium bei ihm nicht mehr möglich, folgert die Fakultät, reklamiert den faktischen Ausfall einer ganzen Professur und verlangt vom Ministerium Ersatz, denn dem obliegt ja die Gewährleistung der ordnungsgemäßen Lehre. Und das Ministerium erkennt an, daß hier ein Ausfall vorliegt, auf den es reagieren muß. Es macht sich die kirchliche Sicht, daß Lüdemanns Lehre das Prädikat "theologisch" nicht mehr verdient, zu eigen. Es ergreift theologisch Partei, wo es doch allein über die Rechtslage zu urteilen hat, nach der Lüdemann mit voller theologischer Lehrkapazität seiner Fakultät zur Verfügung steht.

Mit andern Worten: Es gibt seine Religionsneutralität preis. Ob das noch verfassungsgemäß ist, wäre ebenso eine juristische Klärung wert wie die Frage, ob diese Sonderbehandlung der Theologischen Fakultät mit der gesamtuniversitären Fürsorgepflicht des Staates vereinbar ist. Denn eine weitere Stelle für die Theologie bedeutet natürlich einen Stellenabzug in einem anderen Fachbereich.

Der Kirche freilich ist das längst nicht genug. Sie hat angekündigt, alle rechtlichen Mittel auszuschöpfen, um Lüdemann aus der Fakultät entfernen zu lassen. Und wenn ihr das gelingt, ist der Präzedenzfall da und seine einschüchternde Wirkung nicht zu unterschätzen. Dann darf die evangelische Kirche ebenso wie die katholische entscheiden, welche Universitätstheologie konfessionskonform ist. Auch so kann man die Ökumene voranbringen.

Daß die Kirche, statt kleinlaut ihre aus vorbürgerlicher Zeit geretteten Sonderrechte zu genießen, bis die Begradigung der europäischen Rechtsverhältnisse zu ihr vorstößt, hier derart Druck ausüben kann, ohne sogleich heftigsten öffentlichen Gegendruck zu bekommen: das ist vielleicht das Irritierendste am Fall Lüdemann. Offenbar bedient sie da ein tiefsitzendes altes Denkmuster, das sich ähnlich in die moderne Gesellschaft hinübergestohlen hat wie manche Kirchenprivilegien, sogar im Bewußtsein von Atheisten und Indifferenten fortlebt und sich etwa so formulieren läßt: Von Theologie mag man halten, was man will; aber zur Theologieprofessur gehört das Christsein ebenso wie zum Kreis die Rundung. Diesen Konsens, der weit über die Kirchen hinausreicht, hat Lüdemann aufgekündigt. Deshalb fliegen ihm die Herzen auch nicht so zu wie Küng, der den Gemeinplatz, das Christentum müsse zeitgemäß und weltoffen werden, so intelligent auszufüllen wußte, daß er noch zu Lebzeiten als moderner Musterchrist in die Kirchengeschichte eingegangen ist. Lüdemann aber will gar kein Christ mehr sein, und prompt schnappt, als sei es ein konditionierter Reflex, die Frage ein, warum er dann noch Theologieprofessor bleiben wolle.

Ja, ist denn immer noch nicht klar, daß die staatliche Universität nicht mehr christlich und die Theologische Fakultät keine kirchliche Hochschule ist? Kirchliche Hochschulen können ihren Wissenschaftsstandard jederzeit auf Glaubensniveau senken. Sie dürfen ihre Dozenten genauso auf ein bestimmtes Glaubensbekenntnis verpflichten wie Banken ihre Angestellten auf Schlips und Kragen. Aber von einer staatlichen Universität das gleiche zu verlangen, nämlich daß auch an ihr die Wissenschaft vom christlichen Glauben selbstredend christgläubig sein müsse, ist ungefähr so, wie zu fordern, daß Musikwissenschaft auf dem Klavier vorgetragen oder Sportwissenschaft vorgeturnt wird. Eine solche Wissenschaft können sich die Kirchen in Deutschland nur leisten, weil ein Staatsvertrag sie schützt, und um sich die Blöße einer solchen Wissenschaft nicht zu geben, wird andernorts die Wissenschaft vom Christentum als das geführt, was sie ist: Teil einer allgemeinen Religionswissenschaft. Eine saubere Lösung, die im übrigen die religionswissenschaftlichen Fakultäten nicht hindern muß, die Einrichtung des einen oder andern konfessionell theologischen Lehrstuhls zu gestatten, wenn die Kirchen ihn finanzieren. Warum nicht großzügig sein?

Daß diese Lösung nicht längst selbstverständlich ist: das zeigt, was für ein Ausfall an demokratischem Rechtsbewußtsein an der Schnittstelle von Theologie und Gesellschaft nach wie vor herrscht. In seinem Schatten gedeihen die Verträge von Kirche und Staat. Es wird Zeit, eine Grundlektion in demokratischem Rechtsbewußtsein nachzuholen und öffentlich zu fragen, wes Geistes Kind diese Verträge sind. Der Menschenrechte? Der Verfassung? Was ist das für eine Gemeinschaft von Gläubigen, die das Evangelium predigt, das uns von aller Selbstgerechtigkeit und der Macht des Gesetzes befreien soll, und sich an jeden greifbaren Buchstaben des Gesetzes klammert, wenn es um den Erhalt ihrer Sonderrechte geht? Und was tut ein Staat, der da mitspielt? Die Europäische Union wirft solche Fragen mit neuer Dringlichkeit auf, und die Vereinheitlichung des europäischen Universitätsrechts wäre der ideale Zeitpunkt, sie durch ein juristisches Großreinemachen zu beantworten.

Christoph Türcke ist Theologe und Professor für Philosophie an der Hochschule für Grafik und Buchkunst in Leipzig

Prof. Dr. Hans Strauss

DIE ZEIT NR. 44 VOM 22. OKTOBER 1998

Zu Christoph Türcke: "Im Würgegriff der Kirche"

Kern aller evangelischen Einwände gegen Gerd Lüdemann ist nicht dessen persönlicher Glaube oder Unglaube, sondern daß er mit wissenschaftlich längst überholten, aus dem 19. Jahrhundert immer wieder aufgewärmten Kategorien und Wahrheitskriterien sogenannte historisch-kritische Auslegung der biblischen Texte betreibt und damit inzwischen bestenfalls zum religiösen Anthropologen geworden ist. Sollen die Begriffe der universitären Disziplinen überhaupt noch einen Sinn machen, so ist er genausowenig Theologe mehr, wie ein Quacksalber Arzt, ein Henkersknecht Jurist oder ein Pädophiler Pädagoge bleiben kann.

Der Artikel stellt eine wenig sachkundige, eher polemische Verzerrung der Sachgrundlage gelegentlich im Stil der Sensationspresse dar, sofern es nicht als schlecht verhüllte Reklame für Lüdemanns letzten beiden Elaborate dienen soll. Denn solche immer noch enthüllenden Pseudomärtyrerwerke mit garantiertem Unterhalts- und Pensionsanspruch des Autors gehen nicht mehr so gut.

Prof. Dr. Hans Strauss, Bonn

Prof. Eberhard Busch, Dekan der Theologischen Fakultät Göttingen

DIE ZEIT NR. 48 VOM 19. NOVEMBER 1998

Zu: Christoph Türcke: "Im Würgegriff der Kirche"

Die Göttinger Fakultätskollegen haben nicht den Austritt von Gerd Lüdemann aus ihren Reihen "verlangt". Sie haben festgestellt, daß er sich, ohne daraus Konsequenzen zu ziehen, außerhalb der Aufgabe einer evangelischen Theologie gestellt hat. Unsere Fakultät hat beim Ministerium auch keinen Ersatz für die Stelle Lüdemanns "verlangt". Es hat von sich aus eine Parallelstelle im Neuen Testament eingerichtet. Diese Stelle bedeutet auch keinen "Stellenabzug in einem anderen Fachbereich". Nachdem Herr Lüdemann diese Maßnahme in der Presse als "Ohrfeige" gegen die Kirche ausgegeben hat, interpretiert Herr Türcke sie nun als eine Kungelei zwischen Ministerium und Kirche. Tatsächlich hat das Ministerium vorrangig für eine sachgerechte Wahrnehmung des von ihr eingerichteten Lehrstuhls gesorgt. Ferner hat die lutherische Kirche Herrn Lüdemann nicht die "Prüfungserlaubnis entzogen"; sie hat ihn nicht weiter zu Prüfungen eingeladen, nicht weil er kirchliche Dogmen kritisiert hätte, sondern weil er das kirchliche Prüfungswesen als Heuchelei abgelehnt hat.

Mit seinen Behauptungen will Herr Türcke einen neuen Fall Galilei konstruieren, in dem "erzürnte Dogmatiker" einen Märtyrer schaffen, "weil er nicht mehr an Sühnetod und göttliche Herkunft Jesu glaubt". Das stellt die Dinge auf den Kopf. Herr Lüdemann ist und bleibt im Amt und Brot, was ihm niemand streitig macht. Unsere Fakultät ist auch keine Glaubenskongregation. Ein nichttheologisches Glied des Göttinger Professoriums brauchte ein passendes Gleichnis: Sollte ein Chirurg zu der Einsicht kommen, daß nicht nur diese oder jene Operationsmethode, sondern das Operieren als solches Unfug ist, so kann er, wenn er es mit seiner Wahrhaftigkeit ernst nimmt, nicht mehr Chirurg sein, und es wäre ein Mißverständnis von "Menschenrechten", nur darum auf den Verbleib in der Chirurgengilde zu pochen, um auch die anderen zu Nichtchirurgen zu machen.

Die durch Herrn Lüdemann gestellte Frage ist die, ob die evangelische Theologie eine selbständige wissenschaftliche Aufgabe hat. Unser frei lehrendes Kollegium bejaht einmütig diese Frage. Herr Lüdemann verneint sie. Unser Kollegium hat Respekt vor seiner Überzeugung. Aber es ist zugleich "einmütig" der Meinung, daß er damit den Grundkonsens unserer theologischen Fakultät verlassen hat. Das ist doch keine Bestrafung. Das ist die Feststellung eines Sachverhalts. Manche denken jetzt an den Fall des einstigen Göttinger Gelehrten Wellhausen, der eines Tages die Verantwortung für die Vertretung einer evangelischen Theologie nicht mehr mittragen zu können glaubte und der dann mit der inneren Wahrhaftigkeit gegen sich selbst dergestalt ernst machte, daß er in allen Ehren in die philosophische Fakultät wechselte.

Prof. Eberhard Busch, Dekan der Theologischen Fakultät Göttingen

23

Nur wer glaubt, kann auch lehren

Der Fall Lüdemann ist kein Exempel – eine Replik auf Christoph Türcke/ Von

Wolfgang Huber

Die Zeit Nr. 44 vom 22. Oktober 1998

Weil er nicht an die Auferstehung Jesu glaubt, soll der Göttinger Professor Gerd Lüdemann seinen Lehrstuhl für Theologie räumen. Dagegen protestierte Christoph Türcke vor drei Wochen an dieser Stelle („Im Würgegriff der Kirche", ZEIT Nr. 41/98). Ihm antwortet Wolfgang Huber, Bischof der Evangelischen Kirche in Berlin-Brandenburg.

Die europäische Einigung kann man zu Verschiedenem nutzen. Von Christoph Türcke stammt der –- keineswegs neue –- Vorschlag eines juristischen Großreinemachens. Den Fall des Göttinger Theologen Gerd Lüdemann nimmt er zum Exempel. Er findet es unerträglich, daß ein Theologe, der dem Glauben für sich selbst abgeschworen hat, nicht mehr Pfarrerinnen und Pfarrer ausbilden soll. Das will er ändern; dafür geht er in die vollen.

Damit so etwas nicht mehr vorkommt, will er das Universitätsrecht europäisieren. Und im gleichen Aufwasch soll alles abgeschafft werden, was er für Privilegien der Kirchen hält: staatlichen Kirchensteuereinzug, christlicher Religionsunterricht, Theologie an der Universität.

Was der Theologe Christoph Türcke von solchen Veränderungen erhofft, läßt sich nur ahnen. Doch die Gründe, die gegen seinen Vorschlag sprechen, lassen sich deutlich benennen. Der erste Grund ist europapolitischer Natur, der zweite hat mit der Religionsfreiheit, der dritte mit der Redlichkeit zu tun.

Die europäische Einigung zum Anlaß dazu zu nehmen, nicht nur die Stellung der Universitäten, sondern zugleich auch die Stellung der Religion im Gemeinwesen zu vereinheitlichen, ist falscher Unitarismus. Europa kann nur gelingen, wenn es sich föderal entwickelt. Die Bedeutung dieses Grundsatzes für die Stellung von Religion und Kirche hat die Europäische Union ausdrücklich anerkannt. Deshalb heißt es im Amsterdamer Vertrag vom 2. Oktober 1997: „Die Europäische Union achtet den Status, den Kirchen und religiöse Vereinigungen oder Gemeinschaften in den Mitgliedstaaten nach deren Rechtsvorschriften genießen, und beeinträchtigt ihn nicht. Die Europäische Union achtet den Status von weltanschaulichen Gemeinschaften in gleicher Weise."

Damit ist klargestellt: Das Selbstbestimmungsrecht der Kirchen und die Anerkennung ihrer öffentlichen Stellung werden durch die europäische Einigung nicht beeinträchtigt. Nichts nötigt dazu, die französische Form einer antiklerikalen Trennung von Staat und Kirche zum Maß aller Dinge zu machen. In Frankreich erklärt sich diese Entwicklung aus der jahrhundertelangen Vorherrschaft der katholischen Kirche. Das System der *laicité* wurde auf diesem Hintergrund auch von vielen französischen Christen als historischer Fortschritt gewürdigt; seine inneren Probleme lassen sich gleichwohl nicht übersehen.

Die deutsche Entwicklung dagegen –- auch sie alles andere als problemfrei! –- ist durch den mühsamen Weg vom konfessionellen Konflikt zur religiösen Pluralität geprägt. Daß diese Pluralität eine öffentlich anerkannte Stellung der Kirchen und anderer Religionsgemeinschaften nicht unmöglich macht, sondern geradezu provoziert, gehört zu den unaufgebbaren Resultaten. Auch die Erfahrungen mit zwei deutschen Diktaturen haben den Öffentlichkeitsauftrag der Kirchen ins entsprechende Lichte gerückt. Kirchensteuer, Religionsunterricht, die Zugehörigkeit der Theologie zur Universität, die Stellung der Kirchen als Körperschaften des öffentlichen Rechts haben auf diesem Hintergrund ihr eigenes Gewicht. Die Unterstellung, die beiden großen Kirchen wollten anderen Religionsgemeinschaften Vergleichbares vorenthalten, trifft nicht zu. Daß Religionsfreiheit immer auch die Freiheit der Andersglaubenden ist, hat sich vielmehr herumgesprochen.

Manche halten es für modern, Religionsfreiheit nicht mehr als Freiheit *zur* Religion, sondern nur noch als Freiheit *von der* Religion zu verstehen. Dafür berufen sie sich auf Freigeister und Aufklärer, denen man die neuzeitliche Durchsetzung der Religionsfreiheit zu verdanken meint. Mit der historischen Wirklichkeit hat das nur wenig zu tun. Denn nicht Ungläubige, sondern Gläubige waren in der frühen Neuzeit die wirksamsten Verfechter der Religionsfreiheit. Daß sie sich durchsetzte, ist christlichen Minderheiten zu verdanken, die ihren Glauben leben wollten, ohne von der jeweils herrschenden Kirchenpartei daran gehindert zu werden. Um der religiösen Minderheiten willen wurde die Religionsfreiheit proklamiert, nicht um der Glaubenslosigkeit willen. Kein Zweifel: Auch wer ohne Religion leben will, genießt den Schutz der Religionsfreiheit. Doch darin allein ihr Wesen zu sehen ist verfehlt. Es geht nicht nur um Freiheit von der Religion, sondern auch zur Religion. Weder hat die negative Religionsfreiheit einen Vorrang vor der positiven noch umgekehrt. Freiheit ist Freiheit. Niemand wird übrigens in seiner negativen Religionsfreiheit dadurch beeinträchtigt, daß die Kirchen von ihren Mitgliedern Steuern erheben und dafür gegen entsprechende Bezahlung die Verwaltungshilfe des Staates in Anspruch nehmen. Vom Religionsunterricht, an dem niemand gegen den eigenen Willen oder denjenige der Erziehungsberechtigten teilnimmt, und von der Theologie, die niemand gegen eigenes Widerstreben studieren muß, gilt das gleiche. Wer mit gegenteiligen Argumenten die Religionsfreiheit gegen angebliche Vorrechte der Kirchen in Stellung bringt, baut eine Scheinalternative auf. Vielleicht aber verfolgt er auch nur das Ziel, die Handlungsmöglichkeiten der Kirchen zu schmälern. Mit der Religionsfreiheit hat das nichts zu tun.

Damit sind wir schließlich beim Problem der Redlichkeit. Man nehme an, jemand habe den Beruf des Theologen ergriffen, weil ihm die „Rede von Gott" wichtig ist. Nach langwierigen Studien genügt es ihm nicht, nur selbst von Gott zu reden; er will auch andere darin unterrichten. Deshalb macht er sich die theologische Forschung und die Ausbildung künftiger Pfarrerinnen und Pfarrer zur Lebensaufgabe. Unglücklicherweise wird er an dieser Aufgabe irre. Er versteift sich darauf, Pfarrerinnen und Pfarrer lebten schizophren; denn sie verpflichteten sich auf Bekenntnisse, denen sie gar nicht zustimmen könnten. Schließlich sagt er dem Glauben ab, den zu wecken er ursprünglich als seine Aufgabe ansah.

Ein bedauernswertes Schicksal, mag man denken. Das ist es auch in den meisten Ländern der Welt. Doch in Deutschland kann der Betreffende Staatsbeamter auf Lebenszeit bleiben. Nur damit, daß er weiter Pfarrerinnen und Pfarrer ausbildet, die er doch für schizophrene Gestalten hält, hat es ein Ende. Daß er zwar dem Glauben abgeschworen, aber die Kirchenmitgliedschaft beibehalten hat, ändert daran nicht. Denn ausbilden kann man sinnvollerweise nur die Berufe, die auszuüben man für sinnvoll hält. Das gilt für Medizin, Jurisprudenz und Chemie genauso wie für Theologie, Pädagogik oder Betriebswirtschaft. Daß Professoren und Professorinnen ein konfessionsgebundenes Amt ausüben, steht mit der Wissenschaftsfreiheit keineswegs im Widerspruch; es ergibt sich einfach aus ihrer Aufgabe.

Natürlich kann eine Nichtchrist die Quellen des christlichen Glaubens erforschen. Und wenn er das gut macht, kann er es damit sogar zu einer Professur für Religionsgeschichte oder für klassische Philologie bringen. Professor für christliche Theologie kann er auf diesem Weg nicht werden; daran ist nichts diskriminierend. Wenn einer als Christ Theologieprofessor wurde und eines Tages meint, er könne nicht mehr Christ sein, ist es nur konsequent, wenn er auch nicht Theologieprofessor bleibt. In Deutschland bleibt er trotzdem Professor auf Lebenszeit mit Pensionsanspruch. Nur in der Theologischen Fakultät bleibt er nicht; und er bildet nicht länger Leute aus, von deren Beruf er ohnedies nichts hält.

Den Fall des evangelischen Theologen Gerd Lüdemann in Göttingen mit dem des katholischen Theologen Hans Küng in Tübingen auf eine Stufe zu stellen ist abwegig. Hans Küng wollt immer katholisch bleiben. Wer seine Vorschläge zum „Projekt Weltethos" liest, kann nur bestätigen, daß ihm das gelungen ist. Wenn das katholische Lehramt an seiner Glaubenstreue zweifelte, war das eher ein Problem des Lehramts als ein Problem von Hans Küng. Kaum war Küng emeritiert, kamen Versuche der Versöhnung in Gang – *honi soit qui mal y pense.*

Der Fall Lüdemann liegt völlig anders. Da kündigt jemand Sinn und Zweck seiner Berufstätigkeit auf; aber an seinem Beruf will er gleichwohl festhalten. Da erklärt jemand den Glauben für *nonsense*; aber er will weiter Menschen dafür ausbilden, diesen *nonsense* zu verkündigen. Da desavouiert jemand den Berufsstand der Theologen in Bausch und Bogen; aber lassen will er von diesem Berufsstand nicht. Da sagt sich jemand vom Glauben los; aber um der beruflichen Bestätigung willen bleibt er Mitglied in der entsprechenden Glaubensgemeinschaft.

Was sich in Göttingen abgespielt hat, ist ein Problem von Gerd Lüdemann. Die Religionsfreiheit steht hier so wenig auf dem Spiel wie die Wissenschaftsfreiheit. Da hat Gerd Lüdemann sich selbst im Würgegriff; mit einem „Würgegriff der Kirche" hat das nichts zu tun.

24

Der Mann muß weg

Christoph Türcke

DIE ZEIT Nr. 13 vom 25. März 1999

Ein Konflikt spitzt sich zu. Wie berichtet (Zeit Nr. 41/98), hat Gerd Lüdemann, Professor für Neues Testament an der Universität Göttingen, sich vom christlichen Glauben losgesagt – beharrt aber darauf, Theologieprofessor zu bleiben. "Ich will an der Theologischen Fakultät nur weiter tun dürfen, was ich bei meiner Habilitation versprochen habe: der Wissenschaft dienen und die akademische Jugend im Geist der Wahrheit erziehen."

Und das heißt für ihn: das Neue Testament und andere frühchristliche Quellen auf ihren historischen Kern untersuchen, also Ernst machen mit dem, was in der Theologie unter dem Titel "historisch-kritische Methode" ja durchaus praktiziert wird. Aber eben: Ernst machen. Die Quellen vorbehaltlos untersuchen, auch auf die Gefahr hin, daß der Sühnetod Jesu, seine Gottessohnschaft, Auferstehung und rettende Wiederkunft sich allesamt als Attribute erweisen, die Jesus von Nazareth nachträglich übergestülpt wurden und mit der historischen Wirklichkeit nichts zu tun haben.

In der Tat, zu diesem Ergebnis ist Lüdemann gelangt. Dagegen schritt die evangelische Kirche ein. Der Mann muß aus der Theologischen Fakultät entfernt, sein Lehrstuhl muß neu besetzt werden, forderte sie vom niedersächsischen Ministerium für Wissenschaft und Kultur. Und sie konnte das so offensiv fordern, weil Kirchen hierzulande Körperschaften öffentlichen Rechts sind. Durch besondere Verträge steht ihnen zu: Einzug der Kirchensteuer durch den Staat, feste Präsenz im öffentlich-rechtlichen Rundfunk und Fernsehen, konfessioneller Religionsunterricht als reguläres Schulfach und konfessionelle Theologie als reguläre universitäre Wissenschaft.

Der Staat muß bedienen, er muß seine Finanzverwaltung, Sendezeiten, Räume, Ausstattung und Gehälter zur Verfügung stellen. Aber wie die Steuer verwendet, Sendezeit und Lehre gestaltet werden, bestimmen allein die Kirchen. Das Ministerium zeigte sich konzessionsbereit. Über Lüdemanns Verbleib war noch nicht entschieden, da war schon Geld da für eine weitere neutestamentliche Professur, C 4, jährlich etwa eine Viertelmillion Mark. Auch wenn Lüdemann noch amtiere, so die kirchlichen Argumentation, sei er ein kompletter Ausfall für die theologische Lehre.

Den sogenannten Ausfall hatte die Kirche freilich selbst produziert, indem sie Lüdemann die kirchliche Prüfungserlaubnis entzog, von ihm ausgestellte Seminarscheine nicht mehr anerkannte und seine Lehrveranstaltungen damit zum bloßen Zusatz für alle Studenten machte, die ihr Examen bei der Landeskirche ablegen, in deren Dienst sie treten möchten. Und das ist die große Mehrheit. Bei Lüdemann auch nur gesehen zu werden, empfiehlt sich für sie nicht.

Eine Kirche darf natürlich ihr Vereinsinteresse wahren. Aber einen Professor auf diese Weise die Studenten wegziehen, ihn dann als lehruntauglich hinstellen und Schadensersatz fordern, das ist stark. Und ein Ministerium, das darauf eingeht, ergreift inhaltlich Partei, statt religionsneutral nach der Rechtslage zu entscheiden, nach der Lüdemann seiner Fakultät mit voller Lehrkraft zur Verfügung steht und weiterhin tut, was er seit Jahren tut: Vorlesungen und Seminare zur neutestamentlichen Textanalyse anbieten.

Von theologischem Lehrausfall könnte da allenfalls die Rede sein, wenn die Theologische Fakultät nichts als eine Berufsschule für Pfarrer wäre. Solange sie aber noch irgend Forschungsstätte ist, und das heißt Stätte des Disputs über Bedeutung, Wahrheit und Tragweite der ihr zur Auslegung aufgegebenen Texte, so lange gilt gerade das Umgekehrte: Für jeden Lehrbetrieb, der auf Disput und selbständige studentische Urteilsbildung ernstlich Wert legt, wäre Lüdemann ein belebendes Element.

Wie weit darf die historische Kritik, die die Theologie als Methode ausdrücklich akzeptiert hat, gehen? Den lange schwelenden innertheologischen Konflikt darum facht Lüdemann lediglich neu an. Seine historisch-kritischen Ergebnisse sind nicht neu. Im großen ganzen sind sie alle schon einmal im 18. Jahrhundert vorformuliert worden, als ein paar kühne Geister begannen, die Bibel als historisches Dokument auf ihre Wahrheit zu prüfen, statt sie als Gotteswort vorauszusetzen. Anfangs verbat sich die Theologie solche Kühnheit. Da sie sich als Umgangsform mit historischen Dokumenten jedoch unaufhaltsam ausbreitete – Bibelkritik ist eine der ersten Übungen moderner Geschichtswissenschaft -, mußte die Theologie ein Jahrhundert später, wenn sie den letzten Zug in die Moderne nicht verpassen wollte, selber diese Kröte schlucken. Ohne historisch-kritische Methode kann sie nicht mehr leben. Aber wieweit mit ihr?

Lüdemann ist nur die personifizierte Unerledigtheit dieser Frage, die jeden angeht, der eine Kanzel besteigen will; sie ist genuin theologisch, im universitären

Raum argumentativ zu erörtern und durch keinen kirchlichen Machtspruch zu unterdrücken. Dein Ministerium hat sich da einzumischen. Dennoch war das Ministerium sogleich mit Ersatz für Lüdemann zur Stelle.

Wo soll der nun bleiben? Der Göttinger Universitätspräsident hatte eine originelle Lösung: "In der Theologischen Fakultät mit einem Sonderstatus", nämlich im Fach Geschichte und Literatur des frühen Christentums, dessen Veranstaltungen unter der Rubrik "Außerhalb der Studiengänge zur Ausbildung des Theologischen Nachwuchses" laufen. Das wäre eine Triumph für Lüdemann, wäre mit "Theologischem Nachwuchs" nur der kirchliche gemeint. Aber das Ministerium, das die Lösung vorläufig gebilligt hat, sieht es anders: Auch für das Staatsexamen von Religionslehrern und selbst für das Fakultätsexamen, das theologische Diplom, soll Lüdemanns Lehre keine Prüfungsrelevanz mehr haben. Er soll etwas lehren, was keiner studiert haben muß.

Eine Kirche kann als Prüfer bestellen, wen sie will, und ein Kirchenkritiker muß sich nicht wundern, wenn er nicht länger zu den Bestellten gehört. Aber was geht in einem Ministerium vor, das auf Geheiß der Kirche einen Professor, der Freiheit von Forschung und Lehre genießt und dessen einziges Vergehen darin besteht, die Wissenschaft vom Neuen Testament über die Konfession zum Neuen Testament zu stellen, aus allen Staats- und Fakultätsprüfungen entfernt?

Die ganze ungelöste Frage der Trennung von Staat und Kirche wird damit wieder aufgerührt. Formalrechtlich ist diese Trennung vollzogen, real noch längst nicht. Auf der Ebene des Grundgesetzes besteht Religionsfreiheit, und Religionsgemeinschaften sind insofern alle gleichgestellt, als sie selbst für ihre Mitlieder sorgen müssen. Eine Ebene tiefer aber gilt das Gesetz aus Orwells Farm der Tiere: Alle Tiere sind gleich, doch einige sind gleicher. Die mächtigsten Religionsgemeinschaften sind Körperschaften öffentlichen Rechts, die weniger mächtigen nicht.

Zu dieser rechtlichen Schieflage hat wohl auch eine gewisse gesellschaftliche Notlage beigetragen. Daß man europäische Gesellschaften nicht begreifen kann, ohne etwas vom Christentum zu verstehen, war unabweisbar. Und wen hätte man gehabt, dieses Verständnis zu erzeugen, wenn nicht die Kirchen? Nur was heißt da "Verständnis"? Die Kirchen brachten natürlich ihr Verständnis von "Verständnis"' ein: Von Grund auf verstehen könne man die christliche Botschaft nur, wenn man sie bejahe. Was umgekehrt heißt: Wo nicht voll bejaht wird, ist nicht voll verstanden. Und daraus folgt: Nur Bejahende können diese Botschaft kompetent erforschen und lehren. Und wer kompetent ist, bestimmen wir, die Kirchen.

Ein sauberes Modell von "Verstehen": Es hat das kirchliche Monopol, zu definieren, was Theologie sei, gleich mit eingebaut. Trotzdem herrscht es bis heute nicht vor. Das zuständige Ministerium hat es sich im Fall Lüdemann wie selbstverständlich zu eigen gemacht. Damit ist es freilich nur noch fraglicher geworden. Natürlich kann man mentale Gebilde nicht gründlich verstehen, ohne sich auf sie einzulassen: ihre Motive, Gründe und Gestalten nachzufühlen und nachzudenken. Die Fähigkeit dazu heißt Empathie. Ob die aber die Form von Bejahung, Irritation oder Kritik annimmt, hängt von der Sache und den Umständen ab. Für die Kirche hat dieses Verstehensmodell unschätzbare Vorteile: Es ist als Prinzip der Textauslegung, als Raster der Weltwahrnehmung und als politisches Kampfmittel gleich wirkungsvoll. Nichts kann ihm entrinnen. Wer seine Definitionsmacht bejaht, fügt sich ihm ohnehin. Wer seine Definitionsmacht bestreitet, wird hineingefügt; er bekommt in "Verstehen die Note Mangelhaft". Das erging Lüdemann so. Das geht aber erst recht so, wo noch einiges mehr in Bewegung ist.

Wir leben heute in einem derart bewegten kulturellen Schmelztiegel, daß niemandem mehr erspart bleiben sollte, über Religion, Ritual und Kult und ihre relevanten Motive und Erscheinungsformen unterrichtet zu werden. Wie soll man denn sonst in einem Land, in dem mehr als hundert Religionsgemeinschaften vertreten sind und zahlreiche Subkulturen ihre Rituale entwickeln, miteinander klarkommen? Alles spricht dafür, daß Religionsunterricht Pflichtfach wird und damit aufhört, konfessionsabhängig zu sein.

Man muß nicht lange raten; was den Initiatoren eines solchen Unterrichts, des in Brandenburg eingeführten Schulfachs LER (Lebenskunde – Ethik – Religion), entgegengehalten wird. Nichtkonfessioneller Religionsunterricht laufe faktisch auf "indifferrente Information" hinaus, heißt es in einem kirchenrechtlichen Gutachten, und lassen damit das Enscheidende aus: die Erfahrungsseite von Religion. Daher müsse der Unterricht von in der Sache engagierten Lehrern gehalten werden: also konfessionell. Natürlich nicht, um zu indoktrinieren, sondern einzig, um die "Freiheit zur Religion" sicherzustellen. Weshalb auch sonst sollten die Kirchen zur Verfassungsbeschwerde gegen LER mobilisiert haben?

Es wird Zeit, den Fall Lüdemann als universitäres Gegenstück zu LER zu erkennen. Deshalb muß man Lüdemanns Position noch nicht teilen und schon gar nicht finden, LER sei bereits in Höchstform. Aber selbst wenn beide sonst in rein gar nichts verdienstvoll wären: Daß sie, von entgegengesetzten Enden aus, ans Licht bringen, welch Geistes Kind das hierzulande in Religionsdingen immer noch vorherrschende Verstehensmodell ist, ist schon Verdienst genug.

Im Kirchenraum mag dieses Modell Blüten treiben, wie es will. Überall hingegen, wo es in den öffentlichen Raum von Bildung und Wissenschaft hineinragt, muß es aufhören, die unerkannte Grundlage von Ministeriumsentscheidungen zu sein oder gar von Urteilen des Bundesverfassungsgerichts. Der Karlsruher Beschluß über LER steht ja noch aus.

Der Autor ist Theologe und Professor für Philosophie an der Hochschule für Grafik und Buchkunst in Leipzig.

25

Glaube und Taktik
Der Fall Lüdemann – eine Entgegnung

Robert Leicht

Die Zeit Nr. 16 vom 15. April 1999

Probleme werden immer wieder an Personen deutlich. Aber immer wieder lassen auch bestimmte Personen bestimmte Probleme undeutlich werden. Das gilt nun gewiß für den Fall des Theologieprofessors Gerd Lüdemann zu Göttingen, der nun – nachdem er sich von seinem Glauben öffentlich losgesagt hat – nicht mehr als Professor für neutestamentliche Theologie lehren, sondern auf einem Sonderstatus für Geschichte und Literatur des frühen Christentums zuständig sein soll; allerdings nicht mehr für Prüfungen. Dieser Vorgang, desssen sich Christoph Türcke zum zweiten Mal angenommen hat (Der Mann muß weg, Zeit Nr. 13/99), läßt sich freilich vollständig nur verstehen, wenn man Person und Problem, Fall und Sache klar voneinander trennt.

Zunächst – unvermeidlicherweise, aber nur im Rahmen des Nötigen – zur Person. Wenn Gerd Lüdemann, wie man früher gesagt haben würde, vom christlichen Glauben abfällt, wenn er sich, wie er es selber öffentlich tut, als "Nichtchrist" bezeichnet – so hat dies jedermann zu respektieren. Konsequent wäre es freilich, wenn er daraufhin auch aus der Kirche austräte (es gehört übrigens zu den merkwürdigen liberalen Grundzügen unseres Staatskirchenrechts, daß es einen Ausschluß aus einer Religionsgesellschaft öffentlichen Rechts nicht gibt – so heftig auch der Betreffende abschwört, kritisiert oder gar verhöhnt).

Doch diesen Austritt vollzieht Lüdemann nicht – und zwar mit folgender Begründung: "Ich spreche hier fast wie ein Gewerkschaftler, denn mein Kirchenaustritt würde nach geltendem Recht dazu führen, daß ich meinen Lehrstuhl verliere. Das aber möchte ich vermeiden" – so in einem Gespräch mit den

Evangelischen Kommentaren. Ob er die Absage an seinen alten Glauben hin und wieder bereut habe? – "Nein, allerdings habe ich mich zwischenzeitlich gefragt, ob es klug war, diesen Schritt öffentlich zu machen, weil er zu erheblichen finanziellen Einbußen für meine Mitarbeiter geführt hat." Auf seine Inkonseqenz hin angesprochen: "Ja, das sage ich auch ganz offen: Mein Verbleib in der Kirche ist eine Frage der Taktik." – Wenn es in diesem Fall also ein Glaubwürdigkeitsproblem gibt, so liegt es bei Lüdemann selber, der sich jedenfalls nicht zum bedingungslosen Wahrheitssucher stilisieren läßt.

Unabhängig davon bleibt die Frage: Ist es denn richtig, daß die Kirchen an den theologischen Fakultäten der staatlichen Universitäten ein Mitspracherecht haben? Und zwar so, daß sie – in den Vereinbarungen mit der katholischen Kirche sehr stark, bei den protestantischen Landeskirchen viel schwächer, wenn überhaupt – über den Inhalt dessen, was als katholische oder evangelische Theologie gelehrt wird, wachen können. Wer für einen absolut laizistischen Staat eintritt (und auch in einem solchen Staat haben Kirchen ihren Auftrag, wie man so sagt: freudig wahrzunehmen), der kommt zu einem klaren Nein. In Deutschland ist es geschichtlich aber anders gekommen. Wer will, mag dies bedauern. Aber er sollte wenigstens erwähnen, daß dies eine vielfach bestätigte verfassungsrechtliche Grundentscheidung des demokratischen Staates (und seiner frei konstituierten Parteien) ist – und nicht etwa ein kirchlicher Oktroi.

Die letzte Bestätigung dieses historischen Kompromisses fand faktisch in der Verfassungsdebatte statt, die der deutschen Wiedervereinigung folgte. Auch 1994 wollte in der Gemeinsamen Kommission zur Verfassungsreform niemand etwas an diesen Grundstrukturen ändern. Trotzdem kann man darüber streiten – wenn man zunächst die politische, die freiheitlich-demokratische und verfassungsrechtliche Legitimation des Status quo zur Kenntnis bringt.

Gewiß, dem Kompromiß wohnen Spannungen inne. So auch hier: zwischen dem rationalistischen Wissenschaftsverständnis auf der einen Seite und der bekenntnisgebundenen Lehre auf der anderen. Aber man soll die Dinge auch nicht ins Extrem übertreiben: Auch das rationalistische Wissenschaftsverständnis würde verkrüppelt dargestellt, wollte man so tun, als gäbe es in den säkularen Wissenschaften nicht auch so etwas wie Vorverständnisse, nichtrationalistische Axiome – also die nichtwissenschaftlichen Bedingungen der Möglichkeit von Wissenschaft. Voraussetzungslose Wissenschaft ist keine Wissenschaft. Jede Wissenschaft hat also ihre Hermeneutik, ihre "Professionalität" – und damit, so die wörtliche Übersetzung: ihre Bekenntnis zur Sache. Wer aber die Sache selber für einen Humbug hält, kann sie eben auch nicht professionell lehren.

Insofern ist von der wissenschaftlichen Theologie an staatlichen Fakultäten zu Recht zu erwarten, daß sie jeden noch so scharfen (und scharfsinnigen) Disput um die Sache aushält – ja geradezu sucht und herausfordert. Aber dieses "Sprachspiel" (und also: Gedankenspiel) läßt sich nur treiben, wenn man der Sache überhaupt ein Minimum – und das heißt genauer: ein Maximum – an Sinn zumißt.

Kritische Wissenschaft heißt eben auch unterscheidende Wissenschaft. Und weshalb sollte es so schwer sein, zu unterscheiden zwischen einer allein vom Staat veranstalteten (vergleichenden) Religionswissenschaft, in der die Religion als reines Objekt der Betrachtung fungiert, und einer von den Kirchen mitzuverantwortenden Theologie, in der der Wissenschaftler als Subjekt in einer existentiellen Beziehung zu seinem Gegenstand steht?

Unterstellt man einmal, daß theologische Fakultäten an staatlichen Universitäten der Universität wie den Studierenden nützen können, und zwar auch den Nichtchristen – deshalb, weil sie einen Ort bieten, an dem das Ganze der menschlichen Existenz (angebotsweise) interpretiert wird —, dann halten die übrigen Spielregeln der Wissenschaft das "Sprachspiel" offener als im kirchlichen Eigenbetrieb – zum Vorteil von Universität und Kirchen. Und der Gesellschaft, die doch nach Orientierungsangeboten verlangt.

Es versteht sich von selbst, daß auch alle anderen Religionen in einem weltanschaulich neutralen Staat in dieses Sprachspiel einbezogen werden müssen, sofern sie die minimalen organisatorischen Voraussetzungen und die Loyalität zur freiheitlichen Verfassung gewährleisten. Und unter diesen Voraussetzungen ist es wiederum nicht Sache des Staates, zu entscheiden, was authentische Lehre ist, sei es des Judentums, sei es des Islam.

Eine ironische Pointe am Rande: Hätte Türcke recht (oder bekäme er politisch recht), würde man also die Theologie konsequent aus der staatlichen Universität verbannen, so wäre Gerd Lüdemann längst arbeits- und stellungslos. Denn an einer kirchlichen Hochschule, ohne (was ja mitzudenken wäre) lebenslangen Beamtenstatus, wäre Lüdemanns taktisches Verhältnis zu Kirche und Glaubwürdigkeit ein Ding ganz und gar der Unmöglichkeit. So bleibt eben doch der wenig heroische Eindruck eines Mannes, der in jene Hand beißt, die ihn ernährt – und dafür Beifall sucht. Und auch noch findet.

Reply

Gerd Lüdemann
Die Zeit Nr. 19, 6 May, 1999

Missverstanden

Zu Robert Leicht: "Glaube und Taktik", ZEIT Nr. 16

Robert Leicht nimmt meine Äußerungen dazu, warum ich als Nicht-mehr-Christ trotzdem nicht aus der Kirche austrete, zum Anlaß, meine Glaubwürdigkeit in Zweifel zu ziehen. Er vertraut darauf, daß ein in Taktik begründetes Verhalten unredlich sei. Doch gerade auf Redlichkeit und Wahrhaftigkeit lege ich großen Wert und sehe nicht, warum mein "taktisches" Verhalten an dem von Leicht genannten Punkt gegenteilig ausgelegt werden könnte. Die Zugehörigkeit zu einer christlichen Kirche ist nämlich hierzulande immer noch die Voraussetzung dafür, Theologie lehren zu dürfen. Ich möchte das weiter tun, weil ich mir die Kompetenz dazu erworben habe und meine fachliche Arbeit nach wie vor wissenschaftlichen Standards folgt. Ich will innerhalb der theologischen Fakultät für Reformen werben und beispielsweise auch für die Abschaffung der genannten Voraussetzung Mehrheiten suchen. Um das Ethos der Wahrhaftigkeit zu wahren, habe ich offen mein Motiv für das Verbleiben in der Kirche genannt.

26

Christianity Untrue, Says Teacher
Church Wants to Stop Him from Training
Students for Ministry

Ray Waddle
Religion Editor, *The Tennessean*

THE TENNESSEAN, AUGUST 29, 1998

Gerd Lüdemann no longer believes in Christianity, and he suspects a lot of Christians secretly agree with him.

The difference is that Lüdemann, a noted author here and in Europe, is going public with his disbelief. The other difference is he teaches the New Testament in a school in Germany that trains ministers, and he wants to continue there despite threats by the churches to kick him out.

"People know Christianity is not true, but they won't address it publicly,"

"It's the skeleton in the closet. But I want to get the discussion going. That can only happen if you don't mind being stigmatized."

Lüdemann, 52, is a friendly man with a Web site, www.gerdluedemann.de, and a twinkle in his eye even as he declares traditional Christian belief is no longer possible.

He insists liberal Christianity is dishonest when it does not admit its skepticism about the faith's miraculous claims. He thinks anybody who wants to be a serious Christian ought to take up fundamentalism.

His hunch is that many other churchgoers feel what he feels but don't admit it - a deep disconnection between the miraculous world of Sunday morning

Bible teaching and the daily world of rational laws of nature and social change.

"Liberals are dishonest if they think the Bible is on their side," said Lüdemann, who taught at Vanderbilt Divinity School for three years in the early 1980s and still has research privileges there.

"The Bible is against democracy, against tolerance, against equality."

He has come to embrace a private religion that honors the mysteries of nature and the subconscious. He believes his kind of mystical piety is the wave of the future in a post-Christian era.

Lüdemann has been called a publicity-monger; he's a scholar who doesn't shy from notoriety. He's written several books that question or attack core Christian beliefs, such as Jesus' Resurrection and his Virgin Birth.

He happily appears as the token religious skeptic on local talk shows and national TV documentaries.

His latest book, however, has gotten him in hot water with the Lutheran churches that underwrite his teaching job at the University of Goettingen in Germany.

The book, The Great Deception, argues the Resurrection was a pious hoax created, intentionally or not, by Jesus' apostles.

"Great Deception - it's an ugly title, but if it's true, why not tell the truth?" said Lüdemann, a family man who was a passionate Christian preacher as a teenager and later considered joining a monastery. "Let's not deceive people."

The book opens with a "Letter to Jesus" in which Lüdemann bids farewell to the beloved Jesus of his youth, urging the Redeemer to free himself from the confusions and conflicts of the modern church and return to the first century.

"You proclaimed the future kingdom of God, but what came was the church. Lüdemann writes. "Your message has been falsified by your supporters for their own advantage, contrary to the historical truth."

The "case of Lüdemann" has stirred unease in Germany, triggered debate about the limits of academic freedom and raised questions about the aims of liberal theology.

The historical-critical methods of theology he teaches in Europe are the bread and butter of the most prestigious seminaries in the United States, too, including Vanderbilt Divinity School.

Lüdemann argues that liberal theology pretends to affirm belief but is based on skeptical methods of scholarship that deny miracles and strip the Bible of supernatural origins.

"It sucks the blood out of the gods and in the end prays only to symbols," be said.

The Vanderbilt Divinity dean says Lüdemann is "marvelously" provocative but guilty of "arrogant presumption" if he thinks people can't be Christian unless they embrace every traditional creed.

"I'm a great believer that the spirit of God is very active in the world today," Dean Joseph Hough said. "What Jesus revealed was an extraordinary sensitivity to the presence of the Spirit. His message is that anxiety is misplaced because God is trying to create loving opportunities for people in the world."

Hough said Lüdemann's analysis assumes Christian belief is static and unchanging, but that only puts limits on how God reveals himself to people.

"People are perceiving God in new ways all the time," Hough said. "All those things in the ancient creeds – the Resurrection, the Virgin Birth – are being reaffirmed and reinterpreted all the time. More than 50% of the people I know believe most of that, but they reserve the right to interpret it the way they want to."

Lüdemann is also a member of the famous, or infamous, Jesus Seminar, which has declared many of – the New Testament words of Jesus were probably made up by later writers.

Lüdemann said the Jesus Seminar vainly tries to "modernize" Jesus, turning him into a wandering philosopher instead of respecting him as a first century figure who is now out of reach.

Lüdemann said he still views Jesus as a deeply moving figure, one of the world's great religious teachers. But he argues Jesus' grieving disciples, and then hundreds of others, suffered hallucinations after his death and called it the Resurrection.

One local conservative scholar, Michael Moss of Lipscomb University, applauded Lüdemann for saying what conservatives have long suspected, that liberal theology "cuts the guts out of the Gospel itself by jettisoning the miracles from the story."

Moss argued against Lüdemann's dismissal of the Resurrection.

"There were so many witnesses," said Moss, associate dean of Lipscomb's College of Bible and Ministry. "What do you do with those folks? It's wishful thinking to say they all had the same hallucination. That can't explain why they were willing to sacrifice their lives later to tell the Gospel."

Meanwhile, a legal conflict is brewing in Germany between the Protestant church conference and the government over Lüdemann's faculty position at Göttingen.

The church conference has a say in who gets to teach on the theology faculty, but Lüdemann's tenured salary is paid by the state. In a statement released last month the church organization said Lüdemann had in effect disqualified himself from teaching ministers-in-training because of his views against the faith. The churches want him off the faculty. Lüdemann would remain a university professor there but would be isolated, without students or classes.

Lüdemann said he wants to continue on the theology faculty, teaching the technicalities of ancient languages and Bible text analysis, and challenging students.

"It's a 'scientific' approach to the texts. My beliefs wouldn't matter," he said.

At Vanderbilt, Hough was asked hypothetically if it would be appropriate for such a nonbelieving scholar to teach at Vanderbilt or other modern divinity schools.

"I wouldn't rule it out in principle because he's a fine New Testament scholar, despite some naive personal assumptions," he said. "But we can't have teachers renouncing Christianity in the classroom. If he had no sympathy for our mission to train Christian ministers, he'd have to decide whether he could teach in such a classroom. "

Lüdemann said people owe it to their integrity to seek truth and risk abandoning cherished beliefs.

"Why are we educating people?" he asked. "Is it just a hobby? Are we interested in truth? It's cynical to say that society can't tell the truth to itself

"We live only once. We have to have the courage to seek the knowledge of who we are."

27

Nonbeliever Has an Unlikely Following at First Presbyterian

By Ray Waddle / Religion Editor

THE TENNESSEAN OCTOBER 9, 1999

They're good sports at First Presbyterian Church in Forest Hills.

For a month now, they've hosted a weekly guest Sunday school teacher who, as it happens, no longer believes in Christian faith.

The sky has not fallen yet.

The teacher is Gerd Lüdemann, a world-class New Testament scholar from Germany who lives part time in Nashville and used to teach at Vanderbilt Divinity School.

For 20 years now, off and on, he has taught in short stints for the June Ramsey class at First Presbyterian, a group that often seeks out provocative faith perspectives from the academic world. (When the church took a conservative turn in the late 1970s, the class was banished for a time.)

In Lüdemann's case, faith is no longer the issue. He publicly renounced Christian beliefs in 1998 with the publication of a book that denies the Resurrection.

To him, the modern rational world has overwhelmingly replaced the biblical world of miracles. He suspects many Christians secretly agree with him.

"The secular world is too strong for the authority of ancient texts," he said this week in an interview.

"We have power in ourselves, in our own thoughts. I can't be a slave to tradition."

He keeps some of these opinions to himself at First Presbyterian. There, he focuses on themes of early Christian texts, notably the teachings of the Gnostics, Christianity's first serious heretics. Though a nonbeliever, he still teaches the history and technicalities of early Christian texts and their ancient languages.

145

Lüdemann's relationship with the First Presbyterian class is longstanding. He likes the group's inquisitiveness. He even dedicated one of his books to the class, a 1988 study of the Acts of the Apostles.

Nobody who attends, it seems, is intimidated by his nonbelief.

"You don't have to agree with everything he concludes to find it enlightening," said Alex Steele, a member of the church.

"It's a very open-minded class: 'Seek and ye shall find.' "

Where is God in this world? Does prayer really work? Lüdemann raises uncomfortable but vigorous questions about belief, one attendee said.

"Gerd is intellectually honest," said Rita Bourke, who goes to Westminster Presbyterian but motors over to First sometimes to sit in on Lüdemann's lectures.

"It's possible to look at the things he raises and still be a Christian and maybe a stronger Christian because you're using your mind."

The class is using a new book Lüdemann co-wrote called Suppressed Prayers: Gnostic Spirituality in Early Christianity.

Gnosticism, based on a word that means "knowledge" in Greek, pre-dates Christianity but posed a threat to early orthodoxy.

Some Gnostics taught that the material world is evil, the botched creation of a lesser god. They spun audacious myths about a hidden deity who would someday free their own inner divine shards from bondage to this world.

Their texts were many but they lost the battle against orthodoxy and were stamped out.

"The Gnostics did not understand why God had to send his son to die a bloody death," Lüdemann said.

"They introduce the 'unknown God,' using the language of their day to negate the traditional notion of God altogether."

He hears echoes of Gnosticism today in the idiom of pop psychology.

"Look at Oprah," he said. "'You hear psychological theories on how to seek the divine within us all the time."

Lüdemann, who gives his final lecture in the series tomorrow, sunday oct 10 sympathizes with Gnostic spirituality but says it is too remote from the secularism that people swim in today.

His views on faith have gotten him in trouble at Göttingen University in Germany, where he is on the faculty but is banned from teaching students for credit. He is suing over that.

While Europe fumes over his books, he finds Sunday school teaching in Music City invigorating.

"I see that many people have the same questions I've had."

28

Gerd Lüdemann: The Man and the Journey

Rob Simbeck, Nashville, Tennessee

In his piece for this book, Vanderbilt Divinity School Professor Douglas A. Knight maintains that the German university system, with its contractual alliance of church and state, is set up to guarantee the present struggle between Göttingen and Gerd Lüdemann or parties like them. "The collision course was paved by the very tradition and laws that support the study of theology in the universities," he writes.

Gerd Lüdemann is set up the same way. "I wonder whether he really could have prevented some of his difficulties by being a little more reserved," says his longtime friend Dieter Sevin, professor of German at Vanderbilt. "It would have been easy to, but that is not his personality. He says it as he feels it and believes it. He is not a diplomat."

He is, however, driven, a man who says, "Whatever I do I do it 110%. I am always running, moving, looking, and I have more insecurity than most of my peers, although I am more determined to do things which should be done." If comparisons with Martin Luther are, as Amy-Jill Levine, Carpenter Professor of New Testament Studies at Vanderbilt Divinity School, says, "somewhat romantic," they come up with some frequency nonetheless.

"(W)hat is needed is a persistent desire to know," Lüdemann has said, "which is not satisfied with what has been achieved." It is at the core of what drives him on, and it has proven as unshakable as Luther's "I can do no other." Luther overthrew tradition for the text, although he saw where reason overthrew the text in spots. For Lüdemann, reason and historical research are paramount, overthrowing tradition, text, and, ultimately, Christianity.

He does not wield those tools solely at his desk. Lüdemann has long been a very public figure, embracing debate and widespread exposure. Many of those he knows consider him a "headline grabber," to quote Union Theological

Seminary President Joseph Hough. "It's good scholarship, and what he says is not essentially different from what most New Testament scholars are saying," says former colleague Eugene TeSelle, professor emeritus of Church History and Theology at Vanderbilt, "but he looks for the dramatic." The matter would not be nearly so important if Lüdemann did not possess both a clearly formidable intellect and an impressive record as a historian. "He is such a bright person," says Sevin, "well-versed in his religious field, but also in literature and philosophy. Having an exchange of ideas with that kind of intellectual capacity and knowledge is wonderful." H. Jackson Forstman, who was Dean of Vanderbilt Divinity School during much of Lüdemann's tenure there, calls him "a major figure in early Christian studies in this generation," and TeSelle calls him "a world-class intellect and an important individual."

The combination—intellect, drama, persistence, and notoriety—has had costs that Lüdemann could often see on the horizon. "He has agonized over it," says Levine, a confidante as Lüdemann researched and wrote "The Great Deception" (which he dedicated to her) and other works. "Our conversations were long. He did worry about the fallout." There has been plenty. He is paying the bulk of his own quite sizable legal costs, selling a life insurance policy to help do so. With the exception of his sister, no one in his family shares his views. He has long been the object of the animosity of the church. Friends and colleagues have sometimes been hostile to his approach, if not his reasoning.

Then there are, of course, the sanctions he is fighting. He has been given a shadow position, teaching classes students have no reason to take, with the loss of research money and an assistant. He has discussed posts at other institutions, but even with support from inside them has not received offers. "My direct historical approach is not appreciated," he says. "Once board of trust members hear me say on TV that the body of Jesus rotted away or the like, many of them are appalled." Still, he asserts that ultimately it is not his views that cause the trouble, saying, "Tacitly, many collegues hold similar historical views. The issue is hermeneutics and churchiness."

He has been called ruthless, even a terrorist seeking to destroy theology and the church from within. "As often in life," he says, "though I am only using the force of arguments, there may be a ring of truth even in such a brutal accusation."

The journey that has led him here began in small-town, postwar Germany. Lüdemann was born 5 July 1946 in Visselhövede, a town of 5000 in Lower Saxony, the third and youngest child of a laborer. "We had only two books at home," he says, "a bible and a dictionary. Much of my ambition, as well as my brother's and sister's, is rooted in our family situation with no car and no culture, looking up to others who had nicer places to live and spoke better German." He grew up in a conservative Lutheran household—"Our family did not have enough education to be able to be liberal," he says. His mother, who knew many of the Psalms and much of the Lutheran catechism by heart, "saw to it that our father took the Eucharist once a year, while she, by herself, went to church quite often. What I remember about my going to church as a child was that the pastor was always in black and that I did not remember or understand anything."

At a time when just one in six Germans attended high school, he would be the first in his family to do so. He was a dedicated chess player, taking as a model Bobby Fischer, the American who in 1958 at the age of 15 became the world's youngest-ever grand master.

Then, in May of 1963 during a tent mission, 16-year-old Lüdemann had a conversion experience. "From then on I led a youth group and decided to become a pastor and/or a monk," he says. He read the Bible intently, while at the same time beginning what he calls "a passionate reading of Voltaire's works."Perhaps not surprisingly, he underwent "strong emotional turbulences."

The intellectual rigor he brought to his studies served him well incollege, where he no longer attended church. "I got so engaged in the world of biblical studies," he says, "that I decided that it suffices."

He was demonstrably dedicated. Douglas Knight, who had an office near Lüdemann's when both were graduate students at Göttingen circa 1970, says, "He virtually lived there. He was devoted to working on his degree, preparing for his career. I say that knowing it is rather typical of German graduate students, but he outdid almost everyone. He was a remarkably conscientious and hard-working student. He became fluent in New Testament Greek, and worked easily in other languages. He became familiar with scholarship outside German confines, which is rather unusual among German scholars, who tend to be somewhat ingrown. And he devoured materials about the history of the first and second centuries. Even then, he was a hard-nosed, card-carrying historical critic. He was not at odds with the church in a visible manner, and in that sense the Gerd of today was only in incipient form in 1970."

After stints at Duke and McMaster, he interviewed at Vanderbilt in 1979. He went before the committee, opened a Greek New Testament to 1 Thessalonians 4:13-17, and talked, he says, "about Development in Paul, i.e. his struggle to overcome the problem of premature death before Jesus' Coming on the Clouds of heaven."

Although there was pressure at Vanderbilt to hire a woman if possible, Lüdemann, who exuded what TeSelle called "a quiet confidence," was clearlythe best of the candidates. He was given the appointment.

Lüdemann, who says he was "quite relentless in the pursuit of mycareer," was in an enviable spot. He was 32 and he had both the prestigious and generous Heisenberg scholarship [Vanderbilt was able to carry him for a time without salary] and a remarkable list of well-received publications.

When Göttingen then offered him a post, it was clear to Forstman that he might well take it if he were not granted tenure at Vanderbilt. "Gerd indicated to me," says Forstman, "that he had an all but immediate deadline for responding.

After minimal consultation with the faculty, the Provost and I decided that he should have tenure. I thought by anybody's reckoning he had done enough scholarly research to deserve it." Forstman and the Provost gave it to him, appointing him associate professor in a move that upset some of Lüdemann's colleagues—there was also occasional tension between Lüdemann and those in his field, since he could be straightforward and open in his criticism of those with whom he disagreed. Overall, though, Lüdemann was a welcome addition to the faculty and the community.

"Gerd and I became very close in those years," Forstman says. "We watched their children grow up. He was an excellent colleague to many of us, and he was one of my favorite conversation partners. I thought it was important for any faculty to have one or more members like him who could take any informal conversation and turn it into something where people were talking to each other about substantive issues."

Lüdemann took to Nashville as well, making friends throughout the community and speaking to any number of groups. He had a season pass to the Opryland theme park, taking his daughters there often and delighting in the roller coasters and games of skill. He was well-known as an accomplished ballroom dancer. He played Santa Claus for children at a Catholic church in the city's Germantown section. He proofread the books of colleagues, and was a sought-after dinner companion and someone students and faculty enjoyed talking to over coffee and pastries.

"He is a person who loves life," says Sevin. "He can be enthusiastic about things. He gets interested in something and he goes all the way."

The same, of course, held true in his acadmic work, and even then he knew the direction his research was taking him. His former graduate school colleague Douglas Knight, then (as now) a Vanderbilt professor who co-taught a course with Lüdemann, says, "I remember him saying privately, 'What if Jesus's body decomposed instead of being resurrected?'" Lüdemann, in recalling the conversation, adds, "I knew that I would be spelling it out publicly some time".

He turned down an offer from The University of Kassel in Germany, and then Göttingen offered him another post, this time with a full professorship and an invitation to develop and head an institute.

"The financial offer of Vanderbilt was good," he says. "My decision was immediately made after I was not made full professor. For me it was also a question of pride that you do not remain as an associate professor even at Vanderbilt when you could have a chair at your home university. Göttingen was for me the heavenly Jerusalem because of its splendid past, though Vanderbilt was already and/or especially in the late Seventies and early Eighties intellectually very challenging. Thus the issue was not thoughts but emotions."

Lüdemann's wife and daughters were reluctant to leave a Nashville they had come to love, but his path was clear. He was 36, with a full professorship and all the perquisites at a University synonymous with much of modern biblical criticism.

"I was greatly distraught to lose Gerd," adds Forstman, who remembers vividly Lüdemann's reply to Göttingen. "Paragraph after paragraph after paragraph began, 'Ich fordere'—'I demand,'" says Forstman. "I said, 'Gerd, in this country, nobody talks like that. What are you doing?''He said, 'Oh, that's very common over there. I'm supposed to say all this.' We had a good laugh over it."

While Lüdemann returned frequently to Nashville, where he still maintains a home, speaking often before various groups, he has taught only a handful of courses at the Divinity School.

If Lüdemann had rankled the occasional colleague, he had begun thrilling journalists. In 1994, as his own university sent out press releases regarding his upcoming book *The Resurrection of Jesus*, Lüdemann sent a copy to Werner Harenberg, a journalist he knew had done work on similar subjects. His story in the Easter edition of Der Spiegel made Lüdemann a public figure, at least in Germany, and began the attacks to which he and his work have been subjects since.

Only the extent of his enjoyment of the notoriety is a matter of debate. Sevin says, "I think, yes, to some extent he enjoys or at least appreciates his notoriety, partly because that way he thinks he can start a discussion. It is difficult to get your ideas out in the world, and he thinks that these issues need to be discussed on a broader level."

Once the floodgates opened, Lüdemann was not about to retreat, no matter the volleys fired by the church. "They have contributed to my becoming more and more forthright and in some cases even offensive, if that is the right word," he says. "These reactions, which continue to the present day, have demonstrated that the Protestant church and its theology are bankrupt, which, in light of the biblical record, does not surprise me at all."

As for charges that he enjoys the notoriety, he says, "If it means that when approached by reporters etc. I frankly answer their questions, the answer is a definite yes. If it means that I regularly approached journalists etc. and on purpose exaggerated things, the answer is no."

He was not about to let the Jesus Seminar off lightly either. Robert Price, Professor of Biblical Criticism, Center for Inquiry Institute, spoke of a Seminar meeting at which Lüdemann's book on the Resurrection was the topic of discussion. "(Lüdemann) insisted that the fellows of the Seminar vote on the issue, 'Did Jesus's body rot in the grave?' and a lot of people there didn't want to do it," he says. "They wanted to kind of leave it open to equivocation. One said, 'It's not a New Testament claim and we only vote on New Testament claims." I said, "Acts 2:27 says, 'Neither wilt thou suffer thine Holy One to see corruption.'" Gerd jumped right in and reiterated his demand that we do it. We did, and it was 90 percent plus, "Yes, he rotted in the grave."

Then John Dominic Crossan the next day came back with a damage control thing, basically that just because he rotted is not incompatible with believing in his resurrection. Of course, that was nothing but a theological claim, the kind we do not vote on. It was because of Lüdemann we did have the guts to face the big issue. That says a lot about his unwillingness to take the easy way out. I have the utmost respect for the guy's intellectual honesty."

The next step was formally distancing himself from the last vestiges of Christianity. "In 1994 I still had no problems with the Apostle's Creed and was happy to say I confess with the fathers without realizing that I no longer believed in what my fathers believed in. My historical works had their own dynamics and had to carry me where I ended up in 1998. It was only a matter of time."

He is a man for whom the truth cannot be otherwise, someone willing to follow where it leads. "Gene TeSelle once told me that one has to be open for ambiguities," he says. "I guess not when it comes to the question whether Jesus was raised from the dead and in view of the many forgeries in the Bible." The level of his importance to the age is left to be determined. His sincerity in charting his course is thus far unquestioned.

"When I was in Germany," says Jacob Neusner, Research Professor of Religion and Theology at Bard College, "he would ride by train once a week or so all over Germany to speak in churches on problems of New Testament studies he was working on. He was very devoted to the religious public of the country, sharing his ideas, insights, and analyses, and the people wanted him. He was not perceived as a destructive personality or as someone out to get attention for himself. There was a great deal of dedication on his part to the intellectual life of the chuches. He wanted Protestant Christianity in Germany to be intellectually mature as he saw it. I thought he was wrong in many things, but in terms of his motivation and activities, I had only admiration and respect."

"He certainly is a pious and devout person," says Price, "and he doesn't want to hide behind equivocation. I once heard him say something rather astonishing to Marcus Borg, that even though he did not believe in the Resurrection, he still prayed to Jesus in a sort of imaginative way. I knew then that this was not a guy with an axe to grind, that he is someone who actually wishes he could believe in Christianity."

The list of those who disagree with his methods is long, even among those who are fond of him. Hough, who calls him "one of my favorite dinner partners in Nashville," says he is "a fine historian but not much of a theologian," saying he confuses Christian continuity with identity and remains "too much of a literalist." Hough would agree with Bruce Chilton in this book that Gerd is siding with the Evangelicals in insisting that without believing the Resurrection was bodily one has nothing. "I don't think he's being very helpful or useful," Hough says. "Pushing a vote on whether Jesus's body rotted or whatnot, to me that's sensationalism, which detracts from his own very considerable talents."

"He did not invent this issue," says Knight. "It goes back to Bultmann and others before him. But Gerd asked the question in a very radical form and stayed with it even in the face of church opposition. His point of view seems to be: 'If we say it among ourselves, why shouldn't we say it out loud?' Gerd wants scholars to make their calculation on the basis of their best evidence and their best reasoning, and then go with it."

"There is a kind of purity and innocence that pervades Gerd's life," adds Neusner. "He believes if it's not true it's false, and there's one kind of truth. I wish life were as simple as he makes it. I think he has leapt to the barricades on issues that have other outcomes besides the one he has adopted. And he's certainly closed a lot of doors. To announce, "I'm not a Christian anymore" in that fashion is not an irenic gesture. But then, a good professor wants to raise issues and demonstrate the weight and depthy of what he's working on, and in that way Gerd enjoys a great deal of success. He has made the issues of the early history of Christianity very vital, and has made instruction on them a matter of great relevance and interest. Nothing is boring in the field because he's in it."